Seven Convincing Miracles

Erwin W. Lutzer

Seven Convincing Miracles

Understanding the Claims of Christ in Today's Culture

MOODY PRESS
CHICAGO

All Scripture quotations, unless indicated, are taken from the *Holy Bible: New International Version*®. NIV®. Copyright © 1973, 1978, 1984 by International Bible Society. Used by permission of Zondervan Publishing House. All rights reserved.

The "NIV" and "New International Version" trademarks are registered in the United States Patent and Trademark Office by International Bible Society. Use of either trademark requires permission of International Bible Society.

Scripture quotations marked (NASB) are taken from the *New American Standard Bible*®, Copyright © 1960, 1962, 1963, 1968, 1971, 1972, 1973, 1975, 1977, 1995 by The Lockman Foundation, Used by permission.

Scripture quotations marked (NKJV) are taken from The *Holy Bible, New King James Version*. Copyright © 1979, 1980, 1982 by Thomas Nelson, Inc. Used by permission. All rights reserved.

Scripture quotations marked (KJV) are taken from the King James Version.

ISBN: 0-8024-7742-9

1 3 5 7 9 10 8 6 4 2

Printed in the United States of America

To Mary and Julie,
sisters, whose faithfulness
in suffering is a reminder
that God still does miracles

"I consider that our present
sufferings are not worth comparing
with the glory that will be revealed in us."
Romans 8:18

Contents

From My Heart to Yours

We wanted a spiritual ceremony without it being religious" said actress Cindy Crawford when she wed her long-time friend, Rande Gerber. They were married on a beach at the Ocean Club on Paradise Island in the Bahamas, enjoying the sun and the sand.

Time was when spirituality was connected to religion. In fact, religion, it was believed, pointed the way to the spiritual life. But today millions of Americans say that they are "into spirituality" but not "into religion" of any kind. They want to be left alone with their "god," enjoying the relationship on their own terms.

Spirituality is flourishing.

Best-selling books purport to explore the relationship of spirituality and sex; spirituality and wealth; spirituality and health. There is a spiritual answer for everything and for everyone. No doctrine need be accepted; no conviction that there is a right or a wrong path; no attempt to get anyone to "believe" anything, except in one's own innate goodness and your god's infinite capacity to accept you as you are.

Along with this new openness to the transcendent is an increase in miracles. Some writers insist that we can probe deeply within ourselves and create our own supernatural occurrences. They would tell us that anyone could experience a miracle, regardless of what he (or she) believes, or wants. In a word, the spiritual world is open and a friend to any faithful seeker.

Genuine miracles, however, are hard to prove; often a coincidence, or reversal of events, is called a miracle, yet the skeptic remains unconvinced. So we must ask: Are there miracles that should convince us of the existence of God and His goodness toward us? Do the credentials of the miracle worker lend credibility to miraculous claims? Are some miracles done by the dark side of the spirit world? These questions will be discussed in subsequent chapters.

This book is an exposition of the seven miracles recorded in the gospel of John. Let's remind ourselves that John the apostle tells us why he selected these miracles. "Jesus did many other miraculous signs in the presence of his disciples, which are not recorded in this book. But these are written that you may believe that Jesus is the Christ, the Son of God, and that by believing you may have life in his name" (John 20:30–31). He calls the miracles of Christ *signs,* that is, representations that point beyond themselves to a doctrinal truth.

I've been told that a missionary was trying to convince a drug user to read the New Testament. The man objected, saying that he was satisfied with his lifestyle and not about to "get religion." When the missionary insisted that he keep the New Testament anyway, the man vowed to use its pages to smoke pot. The missionary said that would be fine, as long as the man read the individual pages before he smoked them.

Years later the missionary returned and was surprised to learn that the down-and-outer he had known was now a Christian, serving the Lord. The man explained, "I smoked through Matthew, and I smoked through Mark, and I smoked through Luke, but when I got to the third chapter of John, I knew I needed to be converted." The gospel of John is one that skeptics will have difficulty ignoring, if only they would read it chapter by chapter.

I've written this book with two deeply held convictions. First, *that Jesus was a miracle worker sent from God and had the credentials to prove it.* In this study we shall reflect on these seven miracles to confirm that He is indeed Lord of the Universe, God of very God. His claims to deity and His actions are in complete harmony.

To the skeptical Pharisees Jesus said, "Do not believe me unless I do what my Father does. But if I do it, even though you do not believe me, believe the miracles, that you may know and understand that the Father is in me, and I in the Father" (John 10:37–38). *My miracles should convince you,* He says.

We shall also discover that the miracles of John have a present day meaning for us. If, in our day, we do not see water turned into wine, or the blind made to see, we will still discover that these miracles have immediate, powerful, life-changing applications. No one can be the same after being in the presence of Jesus, and no one paints Him better than John the apostle.

My second conviction is that *many so-called miracles today are either natural occurrences or else wonders done by the devil and his obedient hosts.* Nietzsche predicted that once "God was dead" there would be a "rain of gods" with a shower of miracles. Our own natural curiosity to see a miracle, our desire to benefit from an unusual work of God, make all of us open to the possibility of deception.

To make matters more confusing, newspapers report that there are "revivals" in progress, accompanied by miracles. Some people are speaking in unknown languages; others, supposedly under the power of the Holy Spirit, are barking like dogs and roaring like lions. Thousands are falling under the "spell" of the Holy Spirit, lying on the floor, seeking an experience from God. To separate the false from the true, the chaff from the wheat is not easy, but we must try.

In an age of rampant spirituality we must remember that there are two sides in the spiritual world, and we often confuse the one with the other. We must proclaim with the loudest voice that *not everything that is miraculous comes from God!*

Discernment has never been as important as it is today. With our culture's heedless plunge into spirituality and the accompanying proliferation of miracles, we must be wary of our generation's love affair with the supernatural.

The miracles of Christ speak to us today with new power. And against their background we must analyze the claims made by the growing number of miracle seekers among us. The question is not whether God does miracles today, for He does; the question is what kind of miracles might we expect? And do we have some clues as to how to recognize those that originate in Him and not in His deceptive rivals?

Join me on a journey that will help us find our way amid the competing voices of our spiritual culture. And let us pray that we shall test everything by the only Book that really matters.

When You Need a Miracle

he Chicago Cubs need a miracle.

That's what sportswriters have been saying in Chicago for as long as I can remember. Just think of the Cubs' record: They have not won a World Series since 1908 and have not been in a World Series since 1945. Yes, they do need a miracle. Just when you think they have a bright future, they make you long for the past! No wonder a Cub T-shirt is selling in Chicago that reads, "Anyone Can Have a Bad Century."

I also know a marriage that needs a miracle. I'm thinking of a couple that is woefully mismatched: He is a workaholic who has found a woman at work that he's convinced is better suited to his personality. His wife has been fiercely critical of him, reflecting her own deep emotional needs rooted in her dysfunctional family. As I write, they are contemplating divorce. Only a miracle can restore their marriage.

I also know a person suffering from cancer who needs a miracle. Without a miracle, she most assuredly will be dead by the time you read this chapter. You probably know someone who needs a similar miracle. Hospitals are filled with people who need miracles.

All of this raises the question: What is a miracle? Do we ever see miracles today? What are God's greatest miracles? How can we distinguish a miracle from a coincidence? And, how might we identify a bogus "miracle"?

A few years ago we asked the people in our radio ministry to describe an answer to prayer so specific and unique that it *had* to be a miracle. Many people wrote a personal story, but often admitted they wondered whether it might just be a coincidence. We pray that a person is healed, and sometimes it happens; but in the back of our minds we wonder whether he might have been healed anyway. We pray that we will be selected for a particular promotion, but when it comes we wonder whether our success might have happened in the normal course of events, apart from prayer. We know that even atheists sometimes have remarkable recoveries and job promotions.

What is a miracle, and how do we recognize one?

WHAT IS A MIRACLE?

A popular, but *wrong*, definition is to say that a miracle is a point in time in which God intervenes in the world. God is pictured as standing apart from the world, and occasionally He interferes with His creation. When we see evidence of this intervention, we call it a miracle.

That definition fails for one good reason: It gives the false impression that God only occasionally intervenes in the world. But the Bible teaches that God is always actively involved in the world; indeed, if He were not involved, the universe would disintegrate. In Colossians Paul wrote, "He is before all things, and in him all things hold together" (1:17). Moment by moment Christ keeps the world together; the forces of gravity are His ongoing work. Indeed, the Puritans were right when they called the laws of nature "the customs of God."

It is much better to say that a miracle happens *when God, who is continuously active in the world, breaks His usual pattern and does something extraordinary.* Because this particular event is contrary to what He usually does, we take note of it. A miracle does not happen when God does *something* in the world, but when He does something *unusual* in the world. And the more unusual it is, the more confidently we can say it is a miracle.

For example, we know that iron, when placed in the water, sinks. That has been our experience for hundreds if not thousands of years. The scientific explanation is that iron is heavier than water, so it goes to the bottom. When God determined that iron would be heavier than water, the law of gravity determined that iron would sink when placed in the water.

But one day an iron ax head floated! Elisha the prophet led a band of younger prophets to the Jordan River to build a shelter. As one of them was chopping a tree, the iron ax head fell into the water. The young man was deeply distressed because such an ax head was rare in those days; and what made matters worse, it was borrowed! Then the "man of God," as Elisha was called, threw a stick into the water and the ax head came up from the surface and floated on the water and was retrieved (2 Kings 6:1–7).

What an extraordinary experience! God caused the ax head to sink to the bottom of the river through gravity; then He caused the ax head to float to the surface, reversing His customary actions. So God, who moment by moment directs the law of gravity, suspended it on that occasion. The God who decreed that a dead body would decompose, also raised Lazarus from the dead, reversing customary laws. Turning water into wine, healing the eyes of a blind man, these are miracles that arrest our attention, and with good reason.

A Cub win in the World Series would not be a miracle in the usual sense of the word. Perhaps management just has to trade some players and get "lucky." Or maybe they need a new manager who will motivate the players to do better. Or maybe the other teams in the league will have a bad year, increasing the Cubs' chances.

Whether the restoration of a marriage is a miracle depends on many factors: the extent to which it has deteriorated and the specific events that led to its dramatic resolution. A skeptic would probably want to attribute such a miracle to "natural" events. After all, some rather hopeless couples have been reconciled without prayer or religion.

The healing of a dying cancer patient is closer to the meaning of the word *miracle*. Walking on water, raising the dead, and feeding five thousand people with two loaves and two fish, these are miracles for sure. They are so obviously contrary to established patterns that we cannot help but say: *God has done it.*

What is the purpose of God's miracles? Usually they help someone. But the meaning is always deeper: God gets our attention so that we are invited to look beyond the event to the Miracle Worker. In the book of John, miracles are referred to as "signs," that is, pointers to Jesus' authority and power. Since He is not on earth today seeking to validate His authority, we don't experience the same miracles in our time, but we benefit from what these past miracles teach us. He gave us enough miracles to convince us.

We make a mistake if we focus *solely* on the personal benefits people received from the miracles. Even when Jesus was on earth, only a few people were helped, and only then for a short time. We are grateful that they benefited, but if we think that this was the only purpose of Jesus' works, we are as blind as the Pharisees He continually confronted. In the book of John, miracles point us to the Miracle Worker; they were done that we might know that Jesus is the Son of God. They give us insight into the ways of God in the world.

Given our fascination with miracles, we should not be surprised that there are many deceptive miracles in the world today. While at one time it was not fashionable to believe in miracles, today we suffer from an "overbelief" in them. We have to be able to separate the wheat from the chaff, the true from the false.

MIRACULOUS CONFUSION

Reported miracles today are legion.

When Oprah Winfrey's movie *Beloved* was released, she reported that she had "channeled" some of the historical characters that appeared on the show. In an interview she said that "old spirits were trying to get in touch with [her]." She said she heard voices of slaves—they even had names—and that "she has come to know each of them personally and calls them in at will" to guide her in her work. Before the various scenes were filmed, she spent time burning candles and channeling the spirits of the past. "She would literally channel the spirit of Margaret Garner, the inspiration for Sethe [the slave] into her performance," said Jonathan Demme, who worked with Oprah on the set.[1]

Yes, mysticism with its attendant spirituality is attractive, and millions are trying to connect with the metaphysical realm (that is, the spiritual aspect of the universe). It is a world filled with self-realization, spirit guides, and yes, a world of miracles.

In local libraries, shelves are stacked with books on miracles, telling dozens of stories, such as these:

- A phantom dog appears out of the fog to guide a family away from danger.
- A silent hitchhiker leads a doctor to a school bus crash.
- A guardian angel gets a sick child to a hospital.
- A trucker saves a life after hearing a call for help over his CB radio . . . but no call was ever sent.

I also have read sections of a book titled *A Course in Miracles,* written by Helen Schuchman. Where did she get her information on how to perform miracles? She was introduced to a voice that told her everything she needed to know. "It made no sound, but seemed to be giving me a kind of rapid, inner dictation which I took

down in a shorthand notebook. . . . It made me very un-
comfortable, but it never seriously occurred to me to
stop. It seemed to be a special assignment I had somehow, somewhere agreed to complete."[2]

This primer is replete with references to God, the
Holy Spirit, and even occasional references to Christ.
The premises of the book have much in common with
Eastern mysticism: We share our lives with God; human
nature is fundamentally good; and miracles are waiting
to happen, if we just recognize the fact that we have the
power to perform them. Death is a dream; there is no
judgment; and salvation is entering into the freedom
that awaits anyone who has faith in himself. In such a
world miracles are common.

Recently, a national television program carried the
story of a girl lying in a coma but believed to be a saint.
The proof cited for this was that a statue of the Virgin
Mary begot tears when the young woman was brought
home from the hospital. Other religious objects have
also begun to weep, and oil appears in vases left where a
small shrine has been established. Many people are coming to look at the sick child, requesting that she pray for
them. If possible, visitors leave with a drop of the holy
oil. Some say they have been healed.

Later we shall discuss such claims in more detail.
For now we must simply remember that there are psychosomatic illnesses that are often cured through the
expectation of the devotee. Also, we must remember
that God is not the only miracle worker on planet earth.
Satan's desire is to perform every miracle done by
Christ. We read that during the days of antichrist, "the
coming of the lawless one will be in accordance with

the work of Satan displayed in all kinds of counterfeit miracles, signs and wonders, and in every sort of evil that deceives those who are perishing" (2 Thessalonians 2:9–10). *Miracles, signs,* and *wonders*—these are the same words used for the miracles of Christ! Indeed, He predicted that in the end times there would be many "Christs" who will do so many wonders that they will deceive, if that were possible, even the elect (Matthew 24:24).

Just as Christ's miracles were intended to lead men and women to Him, Satan wants his miracles to lead multitudes to worship him. Not directly, of course, since that would be frightening to the masses. All he desires is that they come to venerate a prophet or a shrine. All they need to do is to get in touch with the "powers," not knowing that behind these miracles is a sinister spirit intending to steer the unwary away from Christ to Mary; or from Christ to Krishna; or from Christ to an angel.

Healings, financial windfalls, and dramatic rescues arrest the attention of an undiscerning public. Satan's goal, of course, is to make people think that anyone can access God—no matter what you believe, no matter what religion you adopt, no matter what lifestyle you live. God is an "equal-access partner." Indeed, angels are waiting to deliver you from trouble, no matter your religion.

We can expect more such miracles in the future. As the cult of spirituality continues to gain widespread acceptance, we can be quite sure that miracles, at least for some, will be an almost daily occurrence.

Let us now turn to the one miracle that dwarfs all others. This is the miracle that God did for us so that you and I can individually benefit from a miracle that changes us forever. This miracle distinguishes the work of Christ from all other religious options.

THE GRAND MIRACLE

What do you think is God's greatest miracle? Perhaps you immediately think of Creation. Just imagine God speaking trillions of stars into existence. If you don't think that was difficult, I have a challenge for you: Go into a laboratory, shut the door, and stay there until you have created something (however small it might be); create it out of *nothing!* I suggest you take your lunch, since you'll be there a long while!

Even if God had just created a few molecules, that would have been an unbelievable feat; but think of the planets, the sun, and the stars and the interconnected relationships they have with one another. All exist because God spoke—and it happened.

And yet, the creation of the universe is not His greatest miracle.

What about the creation of man—is this the pinnacle of God's miracles? Or the creation of Eve, so that together man and woman could be connected with the animal world and yet also be in fellowship with God? This couple was created in the image of God to be the mediator between the world and the Almighty. Yes, the creation of the universe displayed the power of God; but the creation of Adam and Eve also revealed the compassion and love of God.

Yet there is a greater miracle still.

The gospel of John introduces us to the Grand Miracle, the one from which all of our blessings flow. It is a miracle that shattered the prevailing ideas of centuries gone by. It is a miracle that involves mystery and intrigue. It is a miracle that puts the attributes of God on grand display.

This miracle is not one done by Jesus when He was here on earth. It is the miracle that *brought Him down* to this earth in the first place. It was not the miracle of turning water into wine, but the miracle of God becoming flesh. It was not the miracle of the creation of the world, but the creation of a Child within the womb of Mary.

Let's put this miracle in context.

We read, "In the beginning was the Word, and the Word was with God, and the Word was God" (John 1:1). That word *logos* [word] refers to intelligibility and rationality. The supreme Reason, the Supreme Communicator who came to this earth "was God."

Then we read, "The Word became flesh" (John 1:14). This is the most explosive verse in the Bible; it is the one statement that radically changed prevailing conceptions of God. For example, the Greek notion of God did not allow for the Deity to have any contact with the world, much less that He should be joined to humanity. The Greeks believed that a God who was in direct contact with matter would be contaminated with evil. It was unthinkable that God would become flesh. God's only contact with the world had to be through deputies and intermediaries.

Yes, even in our day, this one verse shatters the tattered fabric of religious options. For example, the god of Islam, Allah, cannot have contact with man, for this deity is too impersonal, too remote. In Islam, the Christian doctrine of the Incarnation is viewed as a blasphemous "tribulation" that must be resisted and debunked. This is further proof that the god of Islam and the God of Christianity are not the same God under different names.

The God of the Bible became man. We cannot explain how this happened; the best minds cannot understand how Jesus had both a human and a divine nature, united in one person. The text does not say that the Word was united alongside of flesh, but that "the Word *became* flesh." We simply can't grasp it.

C. S. Lewis agrees that this was the greatest miracle. "Every other miracle prepares for this, or exhibits this, or results from this." Again he writes, "If the thing happened, it was the central event in the history of the earth —the very thing that the whole story has been about."[3] It is a miracle that has happened only once, but happen it did.

Lewis continues: "In the Christian story, God descends to re-ascend. He comes down from the heights of absolute being into time and space, down into humanity; down further still, if embryologists are right, to recapitulate in the womb ancient and pre-human phases of life; down to the very roots and sea-bed of the Nature He has created."[4]

There has never been a descent such as this. Never has someone come from so far and stooped so low. John says, "The Word was made flesh, and dwelt among us" (John 1:14 KJV). The Greek word *eskama,* "dwelt," means "to tabernacle"; that is, John wants us to understand that Christ replaces the Old Testament dwelling place of God. He is "Immanuel, . . . 'God with us'" (Matthew 1:23). Recall how the cloud of glory appeared when Moses entered the tabernacle. This God whose presence filled the universe now came to reveal Himself personally to His people.

Incredibly, Jesus taught that the glory of the tabernacle now rested with Him. "The Word became flesh and made his dwelling among us. We have seen his glory, the glory of the One and Only, who came from the Father, full of grace and truth" (John 1:14). Yes, the experience Moses had when he saw God's glory was now available to all the disciples. John wrote, "No one has ever seen God, but God the One and Only, who is at the Father's side, has made him known" (v. 18). No one can ever see God directly as the unveiled God. That would be equivalent to standing a hundred yards from the sun. But He can be seen if His glory is veiled. So we sing of Christ at Christmas, "Veiled in flesh the Godhead see."

In another context, we read, "Philip said, 'Lord, show us the Father and that will be enough for us.' Jesus answered: 'Don't you know me, Philip, even after I have been among you such a long time? Anyone who has seen me has seen the Father'" (John 14:8–9). Jesus was God living among the peoples of the earth. God could be seen, pointed to, and touched. His presence was now on earth through the miracle of the Incarnation. "For where two or three come together in my name, there am I with them" (Matthew 18:20).

God had to become man to redeem us for one good reason: A spirit cannot be nailed to a cross, nor can it shed blood. If there would be a sacrifice that could permanently take away sin, it would have to be God Himself. Thus John introduces us to the miracle of the God-man, which leads to the miracle of our sins forever taken away.

This is why the Incarnation is the greatest of all miracles. Here is God in human form; God becoming one of us to show His love, to communicate, and to redeem us. In Christ we see the attributes of God displayed: power, love, humility, and even the suffering of God.

Thanks to this Grand Miracle, we as mortals can participate in a lesser, but necessary miracle. We can be rescued by the hand that came down from heaven. And without this miracle within us, we will be lost forever.

THE ONE MIRACLE WE NEED

We stand in need of a great miracle. We have this strange capacity to walk in moral and spiritual darkness and think we are walking in the light. Left to ourselves, we are mesmerized by our own wisdom, convinced that we are doing fine, when in point of fact we are walking in opposition to God.

Proverbs says, "But the way of the wicked is like deep darkness; they do not know what makes them stumble" (4:19). Left to ourselves, our souls are empty, but we don't understand why. Perhaps we have read books on spirituality. We have promised ourselves that we will change our ways; we are determined that we can find the meaning of life, if only we were to get truly serious about it.

We walk in darkness and call it light.

We are sick and think we are healthy.

We are deaf and think we can hear.

We are lost, yet convinced we have found the way.

The greatest of all miracles, the Incarnation, makes it possible for you and me to experience a personal miracle. "Yet to all who received him, to those who believed in his name, he gave the right to become children of God—children born not of natural descent, nor of human decision or a husband's will, but born of God" (John 1:12–13). Here we are introduced to the miracle that each of us can receive.

We can be "born of God"!

Before we analyze what this means, John tells us explicitly what it does *not* mean. First, this new birth does not come about by "natural descent." Literally, it reads that we are not "born of blood." You are not born again because your grandfather was a Methodist evangelist; nor are you born again because your parents were missionaries. You can be born into the finest home and attend the finest church and not be "born of God."

Second, John says it does not come about by "human decision." It is not the result of willpower or human reformation; it does not come about through baptism and obedience to the church. What is more, no man experiences this miracle simply because he says, "Well, I will be born again because it won't do me any harm." Try as you might, you cannot change yourself, even if you are tired of being you. Choosing to be a Christian is not like joining a country club. You can't be born again by human determination and strength.

Third, John says this miracle does not happen as the result of a "husband's will." That is another way of saying that it does not come about because of your father's desire to beget a child. Flesh gives birth to flesh; spirit gives birth to spirit. Human effort cannot rise to the divine level; to put it simply, we cannot do what God can do.

"Therefore, if anyone is in Christ, he is a new creation; the old has gone, the new has come!" (2 Corinthians 5:17). God alone can create, and God alone can *re*-create. When He created the world there was nothing that could stand in His way. But when He "created us anew," He overcame the resistance of our wills, He changed our deeply held self-perceptions, and He graciously gave us the ability to believe the gospel.

We cannot bring the dead to life, and we cannot create light in darkness. But God did. And when we are "born of God" there is something within us that wasn't there before. We have a new nature, a change in perspective, and the creation of new desires. The miracle we need is one that only God can do.

When a father and mother beget a child physically, the sperm unites with the egg and human life begins. God also takes two elements to re-create us spiritually. The Word of God unites with the Spirit of God to do the miracle. "He chose to give us birth through the word of truth, that we might be a kind of firstfruits of all he created" (James 1:18).

"For you have been born again, not of perishable seed, but of imperishable, through the living and enduring word of God" (1 Peter 1:23). This miracle displays many of the attributes of God: power, love, mercy, humility, and justice. "God presented him as a sacrifice of atonement, through faith in his blood. He did this to demonstrate his justice, because in his forbearance he had left the sins committed beforehand unpunished— he did it to demonstrate his justice at the present time, so as to be just and the one who justifies those who have faith in Jesus" (Romans 3:25–26). God found a way to declare us righteous even though we were sinners and will continue to struggle with sin as long as we live. What a miracle!

The miracle of Bethlehem leads to the miracle of Calvary. The miracle of the crib makes possible the miracle of the Cross. And the miracle of the Cross is the basis for the miracle of a "new heart." This miracle divides the human race into two camps, the once born and the twice born.

When God chose to cause an ax head to float, He did not say, "I'll do my part, if you help me, just a bit." No, the reversal of gravity had to be done by God alone. No one helped God create the world and no one helped Christ rise from the dead. And no one can help God create a new nature within us; all that we can do is humbly receive this gift. There are some things that we can do; there might even be some things we can help God do; but there are other things that can be done by God alone. Our conversion to Christ is one of them.

> It took a miracle to put the stars in place,
> It took a miracle to hang the world in space;
> But when He saved my soul,
> Cleansed and made me whole,
> It took a miracle of love and grace!

This miracle is for you, if you so desire. Join me as we take a fresh look at the credentials of Christ in the context of today's spirituality. Let's join the disciples, who saw Jesus' miracles firsthand. And let us come away more convinced than ever that we are in the presence of the "Son of God."

This book will introduce us to the seven miracles recorded in the gospel of John. Our purpose will be consistent with John's own reason for recording them, namely, that you might become convinced that "Jesus is the Christ, the Son of God, and that by believing you may have life in his name" (John 20:31). We will ask the question: How did each of these miracles contribute to the uniqueness of Christ and His mission? And what does this miracle say to us today?

I believe the gospel of John will help us differentiate between God's miracles and ours, between those done by heaven and those done by the legions of hell. The question is not whether God does miracles today, for quite obviously He does, but rather what kind of miracles can we expect? And do we have some clues as to how to recognize those that originate in Him and not with His deceptive rivals?

More of that later.

For Further Consideration

Should We Expect Miracles Today?

Of course we should expect miracles today! We've just spoken of the new birth, a miracle that must happen within us if we are to belong to God forever. There are less obvious miracles as well, those private experiences and answers to prayer that we are convinced have come from God. As long as God is God, miracles can be expected.

But there is little doubt that we are not experiencing the same number and kind of miracles as are found in the Bible, particularly the New Testament. Open the Gospels at any page and there is Jesus, turning water into wine; Jesus, healing a blind man; Jesus, walking on water; Jesus, healing a cripple. Should we expect such miracles today?

Jesus said, "I tell you the truth, anyone who has faith in me will do what I have been doing. He will do even greater things than these, because I am going to the Father. And I will do whatever you ask in my name, so that the Son may bring glory to the Father" (John 14:12–13). Certainly we can say that the apostles did the same works as Christ, but what could the "greater things" possibly be? Even the disciples in the book of Acts did not do greater miracles than those of Christ. Faith healers today, even if authentic, do not do *greater* works than those described on the pages of the New Testament.

This explains why Bible scholars see this statement as a prediction of the worldwide impact of the gospel spread by believers throughout the centuries. These works are greater in two ways. First, they are greater in kind. The skin of a healed leper would again be wrinkled with age; Lazarus would have to die again. But when a sinner is converted, it results in everlasting life. Eternity is greater in time just as an ocean is greater than a creek. As F. B. Meyer wrote, "The soul is greater than the body, as the jewel than the casket, . . . greater as the tenant is greater than the house, as the immortal than the mortal."[5] Yes, an eternal soul is of so much more value than a perishing body.

The miracles wrought by God through the preaching of the gospel are also greater in extent—that is, evangelization takes place around the world. Christ stayed within a limited geographical area; all that He had to show for His ministry was the 120 in the Upper Room. But the disciples and their followers would carry the good news up and down the highways of Asia Minor, across the seas, and finally to the whole world. The Roman Empire would be changed by the message, and so would you and I.

Christ spoke only Greek and Aramaic. Today, thanks to ministries such as Wycliffe Bible Translators, the Bible is available in more languages than any other book. Millions of believers live in hostile regimes, serving God despite political oppression.

Those who are colaborers with Christ have indeed done greater works than He. Christ said they would do "greater works because I am going to the Father." Thanks to the Ascension, the Holy Spirit came upon His people. Rather than two hands, Christ now has tens of thousands of hands, all taking direction from the Head in heaven.

This interpretation of Christ's words is confirmed as we look at the pages of church history. "When our Lord came down to earth He drew heaven with Him," wrote B. B. Warfield in his classic book *Counterfeit Miracles.*[6] This theologian argues that Christ's countless miracles—which might number in the hundreds—were never intended to continue on through the church age. Certainly the apostles also performed miraculous signs, but after their time, miracles disappeared from Christendom. Disappeared, that is, until a few centuries later when they "reappeared" as borrowed superstitions. Pagan folklore, rife with stories of miracles, was recounted in the Christian church.

When the church was first planted in the world, God was pleased to accompany this beginning with miraculous power, but after it was firmly rooted, the need for outward signs seemed to disappear. There is precious little evidence that miracles continued to be performed after the death of the apostles. The writings of the apostolic Fathers (those who personally knew the apostles) contain "no clear and certain allusions to miracle working." Later writers refer to the dead being raised, but never claim to be eyewitnesses to the event; it always happened somewhere else and at another time. There is simply no hard evidence that such a miracle actually occurred after the apostolic age.

Interestingly, there are reports of the dead being raised among the heathen. In an age when medical knowledge was limited, and superstitions abounded, there were those who were thought to be dead and then resuscitated. If Christians had pointed to miracles to attest to their message, the heathen world would have been unimpressed; they claimed their miracles too, even fantastic accounts of the raising of the dead.

A vast body of supposed miraculous tales developed in the pagan era. Some of these have survived in Diogenes' *Incredible Tales of Beyond Thule* and Jamblicus's *Babylonian Tales*. Rather than shunning these miracle stories, the Christian church actually embraced them (albeit with interpretive license) and made them a part of Christian folklore. The name of Jesus was substituted for the name of a pagan god. Thus, in the name of Jesus, bolts on doors sprung open, idols were overturned, poisons rendered harmless, the sick healed, and the dead raised.[7] In a superstitious age, these stories were accepted as part of the miracle workings of Christianity. The pagan accounts of miracles were dependent on hearsay, fragmentary descriptions, and popular folklore. Sadly, Christians accepted these stories, retelling them within a Christian context.

Contrast these superstitions with the credibility of the New Testament accounts. The gospel writers carefully studied their facts and confirmed them with eyewitnesses. The first purpose of New Testament miracles was not to help people, though, of course, we rejoice that they did that. I am more impressed with the vast numbers who were not healed than by the relatively few that were. Clearly, if the first purpose of miracles was to help people, thousands more could have been healed. Instead of feeding five thousand with five loaves and two fish, only to send them home to awake hungry, a permanent "bread factory" could have been established where all could receive their "daily bread."

The simple fact is this: The primary purpose of the miracles was to authenticate the message of Christ and the apostles. Christ continually linked His claims to His works, proving that His intention was not to heal as many people as possible, but to do a variety of miracles that would convince His disciples and spiritually minded onlookers that He was indeed the Christ. The apostles likewise did miracles, bestowing the gift of the Holy Spirit and, in some instances, empowering others by the laying on of hands. But as that generation died out, the miraculous powers, for the most part, died out with them.

Can it be shown that the Scriptures themselves teach that the apostolic age was one of miracles, not necessarily intended to continue throughout the history of the church? I think so. Paul spoke of the signs of an apostle: "The things that mark an apostle—signs, wonders and miracles—were done among you with great perseverance" (2 Corinthians 12:12). Yes, the apostles did have the authority to do such miracles, but there is no compelling evidence that these would continue.

The author of Hebrews echoes the same connection between the newly revealed message of God and the miraculous signs. "This salvation, which was first announced by the Lord, was confirmed to us by those who heard him. God also testified to it by signs, wonders and various miracles, and gifts of the Holy Spirit distributed according to his will" (Hebrews 2:3b–4). The miracles confirmed the message; the miracles were testimony that a new revelation had come from God.

There is reason to believe that Warfield is right when he says, "Their abundant display in the Apostolic Church is the mark of the richness of the apostolic age in revelation; and when this revelation period closed, the period for the miracle-working had passed."[8] God gave us His revelation at one time in an organic whole, and when that was closed, the age of miracles, for the most part, was closed along with it. As John Calvin said, "It is unreasonable to ask for miracles—or to find them—where there is no new gospel."

Of course, not all signs and wonders today are either fakes, of the devil, or otherwise unbiblical. Certainly there are some accounts today of healings, miraculous "coincidences," and other such happenings, usually in answer to the prayers of God's people. Unfortunately, there are also spurious miracles that mislead and deceive. My plea here is for the need of discernment and the realization that not all miraculous occurrences are from God. Nor do we have the right to expect a repeat of the many miracles recorded on the pages of the New Testament.

The strength of the church is not dependent on the number of miracles within our midst. If anything, the church is weak today, not because of a lack of miracles, but a lack of confidence in the message of the gospel. More of that later.

For now, let us turn our attention to one of the seven miracles that should convince us that Jesus is the Christ, the Savior of the world.

NOTES

1. *Chicago Sun-Times,* 12 October 1998, 11.

2. Helen Schuchman, *A Course in Miracles* (Glen Ellyn, Ill.: Foundation for Inner Peace, 1992), viii.

3. C. S. Lewis, *Miracles* (New York: Macmillan, 1960), 108.

4. Ibid., 111.

5. F. B. Meyer, *Expositions of John* (New York: Revell, 1898), 59.

6. B. B. Warfield, *Counterfeit Miracles* (London: Banner of Truth, 1918), 3.

7. Ibid., 20.

8. Ibid., 26.

$\mathscr{J}$esus, Lord of the Marriage Supper

$\mathscr{I}$n lighter moments, we as pastors swap stories, funny stories about what has happened to us in the ministry. Weddings, I must tell you, are often the source of some of our most memorable moments. Here are a few:

- The organist looked over her shoulder as she ended the bridal march, but there was no bride at the altar!
- A groomsman stepped on the bride's train which was pinned to her wig; off it came just as the couple was departing the platform!
- When a groomsman fainted, the startled bride lifted her veil, as if seeing him directly would change the reality of what had happened!

Two thousand years ago there was a wedding that had its own memorable moment! The wine had run out. A shortage of wine was a serious cultural gaffe in a culture where drinking wine was considered essential to the joyous reception. Apparently, the needed amount had been underestimated. And, since hospitality was the center of the social structure, the empty pots stood as an embarrassment, even a cause for humiliating shame. In those days, drunkenness was scorned, but wine was common. "Without wine there is no joy," said the rabbis.

"On the third day a wedding took place at Cana in Galilee. Jesus' mother was there, and Jesus and his disciples had also been invited to the wedding" (John 2:1–2). Perhaps, as tradition has it, Mary was the sister of the groom's mother. Or, some have suggested, this was the wedding of John, the disciple of Jesus, the man who wrote this New Testament book that bears his name. Perhaps; perhaps not.

Whatever, Jesus performed His first miracle, not at a funeral, but at a joyous wedding; not in a temple, but in a home. He was not a part of the monastic asceticism of the hermitic communities. "He came to comfort our sorrows," writes J. C. Macaulay, "but also to sanctify our joys."[1] Here, at an ordinary wedding in an ordinary home, He would secretly "reveal His glory."

Wedding feasts, in that culture, would last for days. Of course, guests would come and go, extending their congratulations, bringing gifts, and enjoying wine. The final evening was the grand finale, and the couple was escorted to their home with flaming torches, walking past the adoring crowd. No honeymoon as we know it; just open house for a week, and time to become more intimately acquainted.

"The third day" John refers to is to be counted from the last event, namely the dialogue between Jesus and Nathaniel near the Jordan River. The walk from there to Cana could have been made in two days, plenty of time for the final wedding extravaganza.

"They have no wine," Mary whispered to her Son sitting close by.

Possibly she had some responsibility for the catering, therefore felt an obligation to deal with the shortage. Keep in mind that her Son had not yet performed a single miracle, so Mary did not know what to expect. Her comment was probably given in faith mingled with both curiosity and doubt. (Whether or not Mary acts in the role of a mediator today, asking requests of her Son, is discussed in the "For Further Consideration" section at the end of this chapter.)

Jesus answers, "Dear woman, why do you involve me? . . . My time has not yet come" (John 2:4).

Discourteous? I don't think so. I'm sure the tone of Jesus' voice was soft and tender. Homer, the Greek historian used the same expression for a man addressing his beloved wife. It was the title by which Augustus addressed Cleopatra, the famous Egyptian queen. And yet, we cannot help but sense the mild rebuke, "Why do you involve me?"

Jesus was giving her a gentle hint that everything had to be subjected to the divine will of the Father. She could no longer view Him as other mothers viewed their sons; indeed, in the future Jesus will put distance between Himself and His mother. She also was a sinner and needed to be redeemed by the sacrifice of her Son. She must no longer look upon Him as her son, but as her Lord. As D. A. Carson points out, she could no longer approach him on an "inside track."

What did He mean by the expression, "My time has not yet come"?

Miracles were dependent on the Father's timing and will. The Father who sent the Son scripted every task He was to do on earth; His life was marked off in detail by a divine decree. Later we will read that no one could take Him because "his time had not yet come" (John 7:30). Whether it was a miracle at a wedding or His death on the cross, every minute was subject to the divine timetable.

Though mildly rebuked, Mary wisely alerts the servants, "Do whatever he tells you" (John 2:5). She knew the servants might find it strange to receive orders from a guest. She also knew that He might ask them to do something that appeared foolish. Up front she wanted them to know that she expected them to do "whatever" He said.

Luther bids us imitate her faith: "She who was not daunted by the semblance of a refusal reads between the lines of this refusal a better answer to prayer." Though His "time had not yet come," she wanted the servants to be ready when it arrived. "Not until the wine was entirely exhausted would this *'hour'* have arrived. All other help must fail, before the *'hour'* of the great Helper will have struck," writes R. C. Trench.[2]

"Nearby stood six stone water jars, the kind used by the Jews for ceremonial washing, each holding from twenty to thirty gallons" (John 2:6). Multiply 20 to 30 gallons by six and you have some 120 to 180 gallons! These water pots, used in ceremonial washings, represented the old order of the Jewish law that Jesus would replace with something better. These stone pots stood as symbols of that elaborate system of outward cleansing that could neither cleanse the conscience nor satisfy the deep yearnings of the soul. Perhaps we should understand that there is even significance in the number six, the number of imperfection.

And so, from those jugs, the servants drew the wine of the new epoch. As Phillip Yancey put it, "From purified water of the Pharisees came the choice new wine of a whole new era. The time for ritual cleansing had passed; the time for celebration had begun."[3] Barclay put it this way: "Jesus has come to turn the imperfections of the law into the perfection of grace."[4]

Consider: The bridegroom failed to make sure that the supply of wine would last for the entire feast. Jesus now takes over this responsibility, just as He will at the Marriage Supper of the Lamb, when He shall invite us to drink wine with Him "anew in his kingdom." This wedding feast is but a small picture of the joys that await us when we sit down with Him, and He shall serve us.

"Jesus said to the servants, 'Fill the water jars with water'; so they filled them to the brim" (v. 7). The servants, bless them, obeyed Jesus' command to the letter.

They did not ask, "Why this? We need wine, not water."

Nor did they ask, "How full will do?"

They filled the water pots so that at eye level the water seemed about to spill over the edge. "'Now draw some out and take it to the master of the banquet.' They did so, and the master of the banquet tasted the water that had been turned into wine. He did not realize where it had come from, though the servants who had drawn the water knew" (vv. 8–9).

When they awoke that morning, these servants, bless them, did not know that they would experience a miracle that would reveal the "glory" of the promised Messiah. What blessings a day can bring! And as Macaulay says, "A brimful of blessings comes with a brimful of obedience."[5]

THE BENEFITS OF OBEDIENCE

Yes, a brimful of obedience does bring a brimful of blessings. These servants, bless them, would witness that Immanuel was among them. The benefits of their obedience are remarkable indeed.

An Ordinary Task Became Extraordinary

An ordinary village.
An ordinary home.
An ordinary wedding.
Ordinary water pots.
Ordinary servants.
And, yet, what an extraordinary day!

This miracle brings Jesus into the center of ordinary life. No fanfare accompanied this revelation of His glory. No pronouncement from Jesus, no flash of light; no shrine was built to commemorate the miracle. No crowd marveled at it. The miracle was subdued and hidden, and as such stands in contrast to the coming wedding feast of the Lamb.

Nothing is ordinary after Christ has touched it. The common water pots brought forth uncommon wine.

In an ordinary hospital room, with a believer near death, I have experienced the "glory of God." Surrounded by ordinary equipment and ordinary furniture, there has been the touch of the extraordinary. I have felt as if I was walking into the presence of God. And I was.

In a poor home, without running water, without rugs on the rough floor, without extra clothes, and with a sick child in the one bedroom, I have seen the glory of God. This young couple was radiant, thanking God for His goodness. Such contentment in the midst of financial needs! Such peace in the midst of an uncertain future! The glory of God in very ordinary places!

Your office, your factory, and your home can become the very dwelling place of the resurrected Christ. Common water pots are filled with uncommon wine, and common hearts are filled with uncommon joy.

I'm told that Ruth Graham kept a plaque with these words in her kitchen, "Divine Service Accomplished Here Three Times Daily." Yes, ordinary dishes washed by ordinary hands can become an extraordinary work of grace.

Think of the faith of these servants! Faith to fill the huge pots and faith to give the "water" to the master of the banquet. And if the miracle occurred before they dipped their pitchers in the containers, they displayed faith that the wine would be to the liking of their master. They did what they could do, and Jesus did the rest. They were responsible for the possible, not the impossible.

Why so much wine? Would they need 150 gallons? The Supplier was seen for who He is: a Man who proved that in His presence the supply is always greater than the demand. He is the God of the "extras." The common has the aura of the divine presence.

We Come to Know the Secrets of the Lord

Obedience also gives us insight into the hidden counsels of God. The master of the banquet tasted the water that was made wine. "He did not realize where it had come from, though the servants who had drawn the water knew. Then he called the bridegroom aside and said, 'Everyone brings out the choice wine first and then the cheaper wine after the guests have had too much to drink; but you have saved the best till now'" (John 2:9*b*–10). Imagine the surprise on the bridegroom's face!

We are invited to visualize the scene: With a jug of wine in hand, the headwaiter called the bridegroom, perhaps in jest, and we could paraphrase, "Most people serve the good wine first. When the guests have well drunk . . . had their palates dulled and are in no position to judge the wine . . . then they serve that which is cheaper . . . but you have saved the best until now."

The bridegroom was equally confused. He could not explain where the exceptional wine had come from. But, John comments, "The servants who had drawn the water knew" (v. 9). They were close to the power and saw the miracle before their eyes. They knew they had poured water into the pots; they also knew that they dipped wine out of them. And they knew that the Son of Mary was responsible for the transformation.

"The secret of the Lord is with them that fear him" (Psalm 25:14 KJV). Those who know God enjoy hidden moments of pleasure that are unknown to the world. They have understanding, insight, and the satisfaction of seeing God in the most unlikely places.

A woman commits her unbelieving husband to

God, and she notices that he has a renewed interest in spiritual things. She begins to see encouraging signs that his attitude is beginning to change; he is beginning to open up to God as a flower to the sun. He doesn't know why, but she does. She can interpret what is happening from a privileged point of view.

A new convert returns to his family, telling them that he has "found God." He knows that to accept Christ as Savior brings peace and a basic assurance that all is right with him and the Almighty. He is ridiculed by his relatives and friends; they accuse him of fanaticism and being spiritually gullible, but he knows what he knows. Whatever is said makes little difference, because he has experienced God's power firsthand. He knows he can trust God with his future. Others don't understand, but he has seen the glory of God.

And yet other blessings await those who are obedient.

We Are Assured That the Best Comes Last

"Everyone brings out the choice wine first and then the cheaper wine after the guests have had too much to drink; but you have saved the best till now" (John 2:10). As we have learned, the good wine puzzled the master of the banquet. It was contrary to custom to keep the good wine until the last. But when Jesus does a miracle, it is always done well. And yes, He saves the best till last.

The devil gives the best first. He makes promises he cannot keep and doles out his trinkets up front. He shields his victims from the coming heartache, pain, and impending eternity of torment. This life is the best they will ever experience. The prodigal son went to feast in the far country, and for a short while he had a "good time." But when his moneybag ran out, he ate with the pigs. Those good times promise what they cannot deliver, and they do not last.

A young man who had a mountain of credit card debt chose to gamble, hoping for "the big win" that didn't happen. As his debts grew, he increased his risk, and with it came emotional torment and hopelessness. One day he pulled a toy gun on a state trooper, provoking the officer to shoot the young man. On the seat of his car was a note, "Thank you for delivering me from my debt." When he put his first quarters into the slot machine, he had no idea that this path would be that bitter, that evil, that destructive. But the devil never shows you where he is taking you; he shows you only the enticing next step.

If you have never accepted Christ as Savior, my advice is that you enjoy this short window of time, for it will never get better, just eternally worse. But for those who know Christ as Savior, this is as bad as it ever will get. Sometimes our heavenly Father gives us a bitter cup to begin with, perhaps the cup of conviction of sin, but its purpose is that we might take the cup of salvation. Sometimes He gives us the cup of loneliness that we might drink from the cup of His presence. Or we are asked to drink from the cup of failure that we might remember that we serve Him alone. But a day is coming in which our fortunes will be reversed: "I consider that our present sufferings are not worth comparing with the glory that will be revealed in us" (Romans 8:18). The best is yet to come.

In Gethsemane, Jesus drank the bitter cup of emotional trauma; hours later on the cross, He refused the cup of vinegar so that He might drink the cup of suffering to its dregs. All that, so that He could invite us to participate in the joy of His triumphant resurrection and ascension. See Him in heaven today, and He will say, "The best is left till last."

If Christ can take ordinary water and turn it into extraordinary wine, think of what we will have in the future. To the disciples He said, "I will not drink of this fruit of the vine from now on until the day when I drink it anew with you in my Father's kingdom" (Matthew 26:29). There is a day coming when there will be plenty of wine for all—and the joy that goes with it.

"They will come and shout for joy on the heights of Zion; they will rejoice in the bounty of the Lord—the grain, the new wine and the oil, the young of the flocks and herds. They will be like a well-watered garden, and they will sorrow no more" (Jeremiah 31:12).

"'The days are coming,' declares the Lord, 'when the reaper will be overtaken by the plowman and the planter by the one treading grapes. New wine will drip from the mountains and flow from all the hills'" (Amos 9:13).

John describes the vision of the coming wedding feast:

> Then I heard what sounded like a great multitude, like the roar of rushing waters and like the loud peals of thunder, shouting: "Hallelujah! For our Lord God Almighty reigns. Let us rejoice and be glad and give him glory! For the wedding of the Lamb has come, and his bride has made herself ready. Fine linen, bright and clean, was given her to wear." (Fine linen stands for the righteous acts of the saints.)

Then the angel said to me, "Write: 'Blessed are those who are invited to the wedding supper of the Lamb!'" And he added, "These are the true words of God." (Revelation 19:6–9)

F. B. Meyer wrote,

The Lord Jesus, on the other hand, is always giving something better. As the taste is being constantly refunded, it is provided with more delicate and ravishing delights. that which you know of Him today is certainly better than that you tasted when first you sat down at his board. And so it will ever be. The angels, as his servants, have orders to bring in and set before the heirs of glory things which eye hath not seen, and man's heart has not conceived, but which are all prepared. The best of earth will be below the simplest fare of heaven. But what will heaven's best be! If wine in the peasant's house is so luscious, what will be the new wine in the Father's kingdom! What may we not expect from the vintages of the celestial hills! What will it be to sit at the marriage supper of the Lamb, not as guests, but as the Bride! Oh, hasten on, ye slow-moving days; be quick to depart, that we may taste that ravishment of bliss! But for ever and ever, as fresh revelations break on our glad souls, we shall look up to the Master of the feast and cry, *"Thou has kept the best until now."*[6]

With some 150 to 180 gallons of wine at their disposal, I wonder how long the feast continued. These people knew they had been to a party! "Even as the Christian faith began at a banquet, so it will come to completion at a wedding feast."[7] The wine will never run out.

Spurgeon wrote, "Fill the vessels up to the very

brim. If you are to repent, ask to have a hearty and a deep repentance—full to the brim. If you are to believe, ask to have an intense absolute, childlike dependence, that your faith may be full to the brim. If you are bidden to pray, pray mightily; fill the vessel of prayer up to the brim."[8]

Yes, we shall drink wine anew in the coming kingdom. The Master of the wedding is already prepared.

> To Jesus every day I find my heart is closer drawn,
> He's fairer than the glory of the gold and purple dawn;
> He's all my fancy pictured in its fairest dreams and
> more;
> Each day He grows still sweeter than He was the day
> before.
>
> Oh! Christ He is the Fountain, the deep sweet well of
> love;
> The streams on earth I've tasted, more deep I'll drink
> above:
> There to an ocean's fullness His mercy doth expand
> And glory, glory dwelleth in Emmanuel's land.
>
> —Anne R. Cousin

"This, the first of his miraculous signs, Jesus performed at Cana in Galilee. He thus revealed his glory, and his disciples put their faith in him" (John 2:11). The word *sign* is used to refer to a miracle that points beyond the event itself to the one who did it. Or we could say that it is a physical sign of a spiritual reality. This miracle points to Christ as the Bridegroom who is preparing His bride for a blessed eternity. He is seen to be worthy of our belief, worthy of our devotion, and worthy of our love.

The Lord of our wedding feast assures us that the best is yet to come!

For Further Consideration

Mary's Role in Miracles

Mary's words to her Son, "They have no wine," have often been used to support the idea that even today she has a role of intercession; the faithful, it is said, should pray to her because she has the ear of her Son. There is, however, nothing in the Bible to suggest that she hears the prayers that are offered in her name. We have every reason to believe that her spirit, like that of other saints, is localized in heaven, not on the earth; she is busy praising God, not responding to the many pleas made daily to her in churches and homes around the world.

"But what about her miracles?" we are often asked. That question is best answered with a brief overview of the role of miracles within the Roman Catholic Church. Since we already gave a brief history of miracles in the previous chapter, we must turn now to miracles within the Catholic Church itself.

MIRACLES IN CHRISTENDOM

In the previous chapter I pointed out that when Christianity came to Rome, it entered a culture that was already rife with what might be called the cult of spirituality. Belief in the Roman gods meant belief in miraculous powers. Indeed, the primary purpose of the gods, as the pagans saw it, was to benefit human beings. In his classic book, *Counterfeit Miracles,* B. B. Warfield wrote, "Men floated in a world of miracles like a fish in water."[9] The more miraculous a story, the more it was believed. The whole population of the Roman Empire was caught in a "gigantic net of superstition."

Christianity was deeply influenced by this atmosphere of unexamined spirituality. For example, the great and worthy theologian Augustine, though reliable in so many matters, actually believed that the flesh of a peacock was "incorruptible." Pope Gregory the Great, in many ways an exemplary man, repeated a story of resurrection told by Augustine (except that it was of a different man in a different location). Briefly, it is said that the man died in Constantinople; the next day while being embalmed, his soul was conducted to the lower regions and appeared before a judge who refused to accept the man, insisting, "It was not this one, but Stephen the smith that I ordered be brought." Thus, the soul was returned to the body and the man lived.

Are we to believe this account told by both Augustine and Gregory? I think not. We should not be surprised that the same miracle is recorded by a pagan named Lucian 250 years before Augustine and 350 years before Gregory. This heathen clearly did not believe the story himself, but, interestingly, the superstitious Christians did! To quote Warfield again, "Nothing can change the central fact that both Augustine and Gregory report as having happened within their own knowledge an absurd story which a Lucian had already made ridiculous for all the world some centuries before."[10]

This account and others like it, prove that Christians sometimes borrowed miraculous accounts from the pagan world and accepted them at face value. Regrettably, the whole body of heathen legends reproduced themselves within the church in Christianized forms. Miracles were seen everywhere, and few questioned their authenticity.

MIRACLES AT SHRINES

Perhaps you have heard the story that Mary appeared to a little country girl, Bernadette, in 1858 in Lourdes. "She was," said the girl, "a girl in white, no bigger than I." Mary had a gold and white rosary in her hands, and she smiled and said, "I am the Immaculate Conception." Interestingly, four years before this (1854), the Catholic Church officially accepted as dogma the "Immaculate Conception," that is, that Mary herself was born of a virgin and was therefore without sin.

In 1990, Nancy Fowler of Conyers, Georgia, claimed that Mary had visited her in her farm home about thirty miles east of Atlanta. "The future holds no concern to those who truly seek God and truly love him and remain in his favor," she told the crowd. For four years she delivered the same message on the thirteenth of each month. Then she announced that Mary would appear only once a year, on October 13. The crowd has steadily increased during the years, though she said that 1998 would be the last appearance of Mary on her farm. A hundred thousand people gathered as Fowler read to them for some thirty minutes.[11]

These visions, it should be noted, were not endorsed by the local Catholic Church, but people visited all the way from Mexico. Many claim they have either been healed or helped by meeting on this location. And even if the help is not directly evident, many who attended said they felt better, more in touch with their spiritual selves as a result of the visit.

What can we say about the miracles said to take place at Lourdes? Many who attend say that the experience enabled them to accept their own illness because they met many that were worse off than they were. And those who work at the shrine say that the people they meet and the opportunities for serving others changes their perspective on what is truly valuable in life. Despite the obvious commercialism, many testify that the atmosphere is one of religious devotion, heartfelt friendships, and peace in the midst of the curious crowds.

Even the most devout observers admit that only a small percentage of the hundreds of thousands of sick who come to Lourdes experience healing of some kind. At least 90 percent of those seeking cures go away without benefit. (As we shall discover in a later chapter, this is also the case in the healing meetings held by protestant faith healers.)

To the credit of the Catholic Church, miracles are not officially accepted without evidence. For Example, the Under Secretary at the Vatican's Congregation for the Causes of Saints investigates miracles because at least one or two are necessary in order for an individual to be declared a saint. The theory is that a saint, after death, will be active on earth, answering prayers and persuading God to help sufferers below. Thus a committee consults with medical experts to determine whether indeed a miracle happened in response to petitions made in the name of the departed saint.

Interestingly, Mother Teresa, who died in 1997, was given a speedier route to sainthood because two miracles have been attributed to her. One apparently happened in the United States, where a French woman broke several ribs in a car accident and was reportedly healed when she wore a Mother Teresa medallion around her neck. In the other miracle, a Palestinian girl suffering from cancer was apparently cured after Mother Teresa appeared in her dreams and said, "Child, you are healed."[12]

The International Medical Committee for the Shrine at Lourdes also evaluates evidence for miracles. Since all the miracles at the shrine are attributed to the intercession of Mary, this committee is not caught up in the saint-making process. According to *Time* magazine, no miracle has been approved since 1989. As medical science and psychology uncover rational explanations for more cures, it is increasingly difficult to name something a miracle.[13]

Of course there may be cures of some sort that are not officially classified as miracles. French doctors often recommend a trip to Lourdes for those who are terminally ill, knowing that this is their last hope and that the faith that one will be healed has beneficial psychological effects. Even so, the number of disappointed people is beyond calculation. Of course, most who return home unhealed do not blame the Virgin, but themselves: if only they had more faith; if only they had done more good deeds; if only they had been more faithful in praying the rosary. Whatever, the higher the hope, the deeper the despair.

To what do we ascribe the miracles that some say

happened to them at Lourdes or other shrines? First, we cannot underestimate the power of suggestion. Those who make the trek believing they will be healed might find that their faith has helped them. Many ailments are psychosomatic; that is, they are either induced or perpetuated by the influence of the mind. Lourdes can change the disposition of the mind and, therefore, also the disposition of the body.

The miracles at Lourdes are much more akin to the healings reported by the Christian Science faith. I've browsed through books published by this religious group, reading one account of healing after another. But in most instances these miracles are those that can be explained psychologically; we cannot discount the power of the mind to overcome some of the maladies of the body.

Second, even if we admit that the number of miracles is much greater than those officially confirmed, many healings are incomplete. If we think that Mary performs these miracles instantly and completely, we are mistaken. When a physician wondered why the Virgin contented herself with healing a sore on the child's leg but not replacing the entire deformed foot, the answer given was that the scar on the leg remained as a testimony to the greatness of the miracle. Indeed, we are told that many miracles are partially accomplished so that the recipient remains in "grateful memory of the benefit received."[14]

In contrast, whenever Christ or the apostles performed a miracle in the New Testament, it was done completely and fully, instantly. It is inconceivable that God would intervene to heal a sore foot but leave the lacerated leg unhealed.

Third, at Lourdes everyone is invited to be healed, regardless of their doctrinal convictions, no matter what their devotion or their religion. At first blush this might seem as a plus; after all, Mary stands with arms open to all, without distinction. Indeed, the benefits of Mary are believed to be the common property of the whole world, regardless of one's religion or gods.[15] It is a message that dovetails with the tolerance of the day.

But wait.

If Mary has her arms open to all, regardless of the god they worship, then we have no reason to think that these miracles are performed by God through Christ. The miracles in the New Testament were done by the apostles, who understood that Christ was the only way to God, and therefore miracles were to be done "in his name" (Acts 3:16 KJV). When Peter encountered Simon the Sorcerer, who "amazed all the people of Samaria" (Acts 8:9), Peter confronted him directly. Simon tried to buy the right to perform greater miracles—miracles of the caliber of Peter—but Peter responded, "You have no part or share in this ministry, because your heart is not right before God. Repent of this wickedness and pray to the Lord. Perhaps he will forgive you for having such a thought in your heart. For I see that you are full of bitterness and captive to sin" (vv. 21–23). Your doctrine and the condition of your heart are essential if you want to see miracles.

Let us not overlook the fact that when the Israelites worshiped the pagan goddess Tamaz, whom they called "the queen of heaven" (Jeremiah 44:17 NASB), they insisted that it was she who gave them crops and food. In fact, they had the audacity to say, "But since we stopped burning sacrifices to the queen of heaven and pouring out drink offerings to her, we have lacked everything and have met our end by the sword and by famine" (v. 18 NASB). The Israelites were convinced that their prayers to a pagan goddess paid dividends; they were better off because of their false worship.

God would have none of it and told them that such worship was an abomination. But mark it well: It is possible to benefit from false worship; it is possible to claim miracles of provision and help. But even such "miracles" do not justify wrong doctrines. Remember that our only hope of interpreting a miracle correctly involves a careful study of the doctrinal context in which it is performed.

In his book *Expect a Miracle,* Dan Wakefield records that his search for miracles led him to many different shrines and many different religions. He discovered that every religion has its miracles. Buddhism has stories of "Tara healing people. . . . [In] times of despair you can call on her and she reaches out and comes to the rescue."[16] The Hindus have visions, encounters, rituals, and miracles. He quotes the *Washington Post* report that the power of prayer is gaining validity in helping the sick recover. Interestingly, regardless of the religion or deity, the beneficial effects are about the same.[17] Clearly, we need biblical discernment in this age rife with miracles.

The Bible does not sanction miracles performed by just any person or any god. To say that it does not matter what you believe is to say that it does not matter in whose name you are healed. Indeed, even those who performed miracles in the name of Christ were excluded from heaven because they did not understand their need of redemption (Matthew 7:21–22). I must say it again: *Not everything that is miraculous is from God.*

CHRIST VS. MARY

On a plane I met a group of people en route to Europe to visit various places where "Mary sightings" have occurred. They insisted, first, that in these places authentic apparitions of Mary had occurred; and, second, that these sightings, with their attendant miracles, in no way detracted from the miracles of Christ. Let Christ do His miracles and let His mother do hers.

But the matter is not that simple.

First, contrary to Catholic protests, this pursuit of the miraculous Mary "sightings" does detract from Christ. It is based on the assumption that the miracles of Christ are insufficient; we must follow some other miracle worker. It is a scandal beyond irony that millions of people flock to shrines of Mary with more hope, more anticipation, and more confidence than they have when they open the Bible.

I have visited the shrine of Guadalupe in Mexico and have seen crowds crawl with bleeding knees for hundreds of yards, approaching the shrine with the hope that they will win the favor of the Virgin Mary. Many are women with infants in their arms, hoping to appease her. In Mexico, a form of Christianity blends nicely with pagan superstitions and legends.

Perhaps the argument could be made that this is not actually Catholicism, but a blend of Catholicism and pagan superstitions. Yet, interestingly, official Catholicism does not condemn these heretical beliefs and practices. Indeed the Pope performed mass at the shrine in 1999 without a single word of rebuke for the superstitions, paganism, and commercialism they encourage.

Second, since these healings, if they occur, fall into the same category as those of the Christian Science religion or the New Age Movement, we must raise the possibility that Satan might be at work as well. We know that he will appear in whatever form he is expected. If you are Catholic, he will appear as Mary; if you are Protestant, he will appear as Jesus; and if you are a Hindu, he will appear as Krishna. To put it simply, either miracles are based on Christ and the Bible, or else they connect us with the world of the occult, with its deceptions and demons. There are, after all, only two "miracle workers" in the universe.

The Catholic Church itself recognizes the possibility of deception. We can do no better than to accept the counsel of Ignatius Loyola, who, when consulted about a young man who claimed that the wounds of Christ miraculously appeared in his hands, said that these marks "might just as well have been the work of the devil as of God."[18] Agreed.

NOTES

1. J. C. Macaulay, *Expository Commentary on John* 2d ed. (Chicago: Moody, 1978), 33.

2. Richard C. Trench, *Notes on the Miracles of our Lord* (Old Tappan, N.J.: Revell, 1953), 113.

3. Philip Yancey, *The Jesus I Never Knew* (Grand Rapids: Zondervan, 1995), 169.

4. William Barclay, *The Gospel of John,* 2d ed., 2 vols., Daily Study Bible (Philadelphia: Westminster, 1955; Edinburgh: Saint Andrews, 1965), 1:89.

5. Macaulay, *Expository Commentary on John,* 35.

6. F. B. Meyer, *The Gospel of John* (Grand Rapids: Zondervan, 1950), 54..

7. Michael Card, *The Parable of Joy* (Nashville: Nelson, 1995), 26.

8. Charles Haddon Spurgeon, *The Treasury of the Bible* (Grand Rapids: Zondervan, 1962), 2:262.

9. B. B. Warfield, *Counterfeit Miracles* (1918; reprint, London: Banner of Truth, 1972), 75.

10. Ibid., 82.

11. *Chicago Sun-Times*, 14 October 1998.

12. *Chicago Sun-Times*, 1 March 1999.

13. "Modern Miracles Have Strict Rules," *Time,* 10 April 1995, 74.

14. Warfield, *Counterfeit Miracles,* 108.

15. Ibid., 124.

16. Dan Wakefield, *Expect a Miracle* (San Francisco, Harper, 1995), 30–31.

17. Ibid., 20.

18. Ignatius Loyola, quoted in Warfield, *Counterfeit Miracles,* 85.

Jesus, Lord of Time and Distance

Somewhere I read a story about church members who told the owner of a bar that they were praying that his building would be struck by lightning. A few weeks later, a thunderstorm engulfed the community and the bar was struck with lightning and burned to the ground. The bar owner filed a lawsuit against the church, arguing that the church members were to be blamed for the loss. The Christians in turn hired a lawyer, who argued that they were not responsible for what happened. The judge reported that the case was somewhat confusing, but he was convinced of one thing: The bar owner believed in prayer, whereas the Christians didn't!

Have you ever had an answer to prayer that was so specific that the answer *had* to be a miracle? We often receive answers to our prayers, but we are tempted to give them alternate explanations. We chalk it all up to coincidence or even a stroke of "luck."

What would it take for you to *believe?*

The apostle John records a healing that was so specific, so unique, that it can only be explained as a miracle. It is a story that invites questions about faith healing; it is a miracle that leads us to believe that Jesus is sovereign, not just when He is physically present, but even when He is at a distance bodily. It is a miracle of time and space. It is a miracle that can have no rational explanation.

> Once more he visited Cana in Galilee, where he had turned the water into wine. And there was a certain royal official whose son lay sick at Capernaum. When this man heard that Jesus had arrived in Galilee from Judea, he went to him and begged him to come and heal his son, who was close to death.
>
> "Unless you people see miraculous signs and wonders," Jesus told him, "you will never believe."
>
> The royal official said, "Sir, come down before my child dies."
>
> Jesus replied, "You may go. Your son will live."
>
> The man took Jesus at his word and departed. While he was still on the way, his servants met him with the news that his boy was living. When he inquired as to the time when his son got better, they said to him, "The fever left him yesterday at the seventh hour."
>
> Then the father realized that this was the exact time at which Jesus had said to him, "Your son will live." So he and all his household believed.
>
> This was the second miraculous sign that Jesus performed, having come from Judea to Galilee. (John 4:46–54)

This is not, by the way, the same story as that of the centurion, who had a servant at the point of death (Matthew 8:5–13). The circumstances and healing were similar, but the accounts differ in many respects. Also, when John calls this "the second miracle," he means it was the second miracle Jesus did in the Galilee area. We have reason to believe that after He turned water into wine, He visited Jerusalem, where other miracles were performed. But He returned here, receiving an enthusiastic reception among the Galileans.

Who was this man whose son needed a miracle? He was a royal official, a man of high standing in the court of Herod. He was possibly a Gentile, someone who was regarded as an outsider, excluded from the Jewish covenants. And yet his faith delighted the heart of Jesus, and a miracle took place in his home.

This man teaches us how faith is developed. Like a garden that needs certain ingredients, so our faith grows in the soil of difficulty and need. In his *Bible Exposition Commentary,* Warren Wiersbe lists the steps this man took as he grew in his faith. Let's take these steps together, learning all we can from his journey.[1]

STEPS TO A GROWING FAITH

Sickness finds its way into the castle as well as the hovel. A Spanish proverb says, "There is no home without its hush." Here was a royal official with a dying son. And yet this crisis led him into direct contact with Jesus. C. S. Lewis, you will recall, says that God speaks to us in our health but "shouts to us in our pain." With a son on the verge of death, the man was hearing the voice of God quite clearly.

And now for the steps toward a growing faith.

A Crisis Faith

With his son's fever on the rise, the man had one desire, and that was to get the news to Jesus and persuade Him to come to his home and cure the boy. He journeyed twenty miles, perhaps on horseback, found Jesus, and, we read, "begged him to come and heal his son, who was close to death" (John 4:47).

Only desperate people pray. When sickness comes, the first step in our culture is to go to a doctor, and if that is unsuccessful, to try alternative medicine. "Miracle cures" are popular and lucrative. Satan was quite right when he said, "A man will give all he has for his own life" (Job 2:4). A minister who had a brain tumor told me that well-meaning friends sent him more than two hundred different prescriptions and cures. He just filed them, knowing that he would not even have time to read them, much less do as they prescribed.

If the cures don't work, then prayer—*desperate* prayer—usually follows. Recently, a woman told me that her father, who had abandoned the family, wanted to be reunited with his children now that he was about to die. In fact, he even confided that it would be fine if someone offered a prayer for him, something he despised when he was feeling well. Desperation turns the heart toward God. In our need we cling to God like a drowning man clings to a rope.

Crisis faith is a desperate faith. It is a faith that grasps onto hope and reaches out to unfamiliar people and procedures. A crisis faith will pay any price and make any promise in order to be heard. Those indifferent souls who have been able to avoid a God thought for years are suddenly confronted with a "quaking of the foundations."

They find themselves thinking of eternity, not time; of heaven, not earth. Sickness can have a purifying power, for at last we are prepared to take ultimate issues seriously.

A crisis faith is also a focused faith. Usually it has only one request, one urgent desire. This father begged for Jesus to come to his home and touch his dying son. He believed that this Man was a miracle worker, and if only He were to come to his home, his son's fever would subside. Diseases flee in the presence of Jesus.

The royal official made two honest mistakes. First, he thought Jesus would have to be present to heal his son; second, he believed that if his son were to die, Jesus' intervention would be too late. Jesus responded, "Unless you people see miraculous signs and wonders, . . . you will never believe" (John 4:48). He was saying, "Why do you think I need to come into your house in order for the healing to take place? Aren't you demanding signs and wonders before you will put the boy's care into my hands?" A faith that is dependent on signs and wonders is not a complete faith. (A discussion of the present day Signs and Wonders Movement is found in the "For Further Consideration" section in this chapter.)

However, it is possible that Jesus' mild rebuke was not so much directed at the man as at those who were listening. In Greek it is clear that Jesus does not use the singular *you*, but the plural *ye*, or as our friends say in the South, *y'all*. Those who were listening to this conversation were the real sign seekers.

The man would not be put off by arguing about signs and wonders. Those discussions could be left for the theologians. He just wanted Jesus to come to his home so that his child would live. Theological niceties have their place, but not when a child is dying and every minute is precious. He was desperate and pleaded for mercy.

That was faith born of a crisis. But it now graduates to the next step.

A Confident Faith

"Jesus replied, 'You may go. Your son will live.' The man took Jesus at his word and departed" (v. 50).

Keep in mind that this was a specific promise given to a specific man at a specific time in history. We cannot generalize the words of Christ and apply them to ourselves. In other words, we cannot insist that if we "go our way" our sick child or we will be healed. Our danger is to believe promises that do not apply to us and thus conclude that God is not as good as His word. I know some Christians who have become bitter, believing that God had deceived them because they were not healed or helped in response to desperate prayers. They thought they had a promise from God, and He was obligated to heal them or bless them financially.

Keep in mind that there are three different kinds of promises in the Bible. First, there are general promises given to all people: "For God so loved the world that he gave his one and only Son, that whoever believes in him shall not perish but have eternal life" (John 3:16). Such promises invite all to believe, and they apply without distinction.

Second, there are promises that apply only to believers. "Keep your lives free from the love of money and be content with what you have, because God has said, 'Never will I leave you; never will I forsake you.' So we say with confidence, 'The Lord is my helper; I will not be afraid. What can man do to me?'" (Hebrews 13:5–6). Included also are promises such as "We know that in all things God works for the good of those who love him, who have been called according to his purpose" (Romans 8:28).

Finally, there are also specific promises that apply only to the individuals to whom they were given. Abraham was promised that his name would be great (Genesis 12:2); David was promised that calamity would come to his household and that the child Bathsheba bore would die (2 Samuel 12:11–14). And in this story in John 4, the father was promised that his son would be restored. But such promises are not for us.

In another chapter we shall show in more detail that there is no universal promise of divine healing. If there were, we would never have to die, for we would just keep "claiming the promise." We simply do not know whether it is God's will to heal a particular person at a particular time. This man, bless him, was given a specific promise: "You may go. Your son will live" (John 4:50).

We commend him for implicit faith: "The man took Jesus at his word and departed" (v. 50). Confident faith is free of anxiety. The man might have argued, saying, "How do I know that when I return home my child will be healed?" He could have asked for a sign or a wonder. But, bless him, if Jesus said it, that settled it.

He left without a sign to strengthen his faith. There was no light in the sky, no out-of-body experience, no angel to accompany him, no feelings, no word of knowledge. He believed the bare words of Jesus, convinced that He who spoke would do as promised. Jesus did not have to come to his house in order for his son to be healed.

Distance has no meaning in the presence of the Eternal. Most faith healers would not claim that they can "heal at a distance," though many of them have encouraged their supporters to touch their radios or TV sets to "make contact." But none have the authority to say, "You may go. Your son will live."

Don't miss the contrast between this official's rush to Cana to seek Jesus' help and his leisurely stroll home. Since the miracle took place at the seventh hour (one o'clock in the afternoon Jewish time), he could have made it home the same day, particularly if he had a horse. But he arrived the next day, spending the night en route. Perhaps—and we must say *perhaps,* since we don't know for sure—he took his time because he was so confident that his son would be well when he arrived.

The faith he brought home was a different faith than he brought to Jesus. Macaulay says, "It was a tested faith, a sifted faith, an intelligent and victorious faith."[2]

> 'Tis so sweet to trust in Jesus,
> Just to take Him at His word;
> Just to rest upon His promise;
> Just to know, "Thus saith the Lord."
> Louisa M.R. Stead

A Confirmed Faith

Before he arrived home, his servants met him with the news that his boy was well. Yet, for all of his faith, notice how cautiously he asked the question, "When did the boy begin to improve?" Maybe he expected that the boy had a gradual healing. "The fever left him yesterday at the seventh hour," they told him (v. 52). Whether hours were calculated according to the Roman or Jewish method, the hour matched his encounter with Jesus. He had an answer so specific that neither he nor his family could doubt.

When Jesus turned water into wine, it was a miracle of *time*. Fact is, He is always turning water into wine, though He usually uses a growing season to do it. Come with me to the vineyards of California or France and you will see how Jesus turns water into wine. At the wedding in Cana, He simply speeded up the process. He did in a moment what He usually takes months to accomplish.

The healing of this man's son was a miracle of *space*. Jesus healed a boy who was twenty miles away. Jesus was not any less in the man's house in Capernaum just because He was actually standing in Cana. The physical presence of Christ does not make Him more present. Indeed, when He promised the Holy Spirit to His disciples, He told them, "It is for your good that I am going away" (John 16:7) because the Counselor (Comforter, KJV) would come and be with them and in them. Jesus could only be in one place at one time with His earthly body; but by His Spirit He would indwell His people throughout the world.

Two healings took place that day. The father's weak faith was made strong, and the boy's weak body became well. All in the presence of Jesus.

Yet the father needed to take one more step.

A Contagious Faith

The father's faith soon became the faith of his family and servants. "So he and all his household believed" (John 4:53). What did they believe? Surely John wants us to understand that they believed more than simply that a child was healed; that was obvious enough. They "believed" that Jesus was the Son of God, the Author of our salvation. Though the content of their faith was limited, we have reason to think that this household will be in heaven, having accepted what they knew about Jesus. The One who spoke their son well is the One who spoke their sins away. He who can heal the body can also heal the soul.

Faith is contagious. The idea that Jesus, a Jew, was accepted by this Gentile as Lord and Savior was unthinkable at the time. It would not be easy for this man to profess faith in Christ in the court of Herod. But facts are facts. He had seen and experienced what Jesus could do. And he believed.

He came seeking a physical healing; God gave him spiritual healing. We often think that our body is more important than our soul, but our soul is eternal and can exist quite apart from the body. Keep in mind that this boy eventually died anyway; even faith healers die. The best a miracle can do is to postpone the inevitable. Only the salvation of a soul is an eternal miracle.

Like turning water into wine, this miracle was largely private. No one but the disciples and servants knew that the wine came from the pots of water; no one but this official and his family knew about the boy's recovery. John, who recorded this story, probably heard the details from the official himself. For now, Jesus was working quietly, doing his Father's will in the presence of those who surrounded Him.

Miracles can build faith. But Jesus' words also remind us that great faith can survive without miracles. Years ago, I knew a missionary couple who served in China before the Communist takeover of 1949. They had lived high in the hills, and their only means of transportation was using a boat on a nearby river. At a particular time of year the river was dried up.

One day their child was ill with a high fever. They knew that if they were to get medical help, they would have to travel by boat, but the river was only a muddy stream. They prayed that it would rain so that the river would swell and their boat would travel. But their prayers were not answered. Days later, their child died.

Shortly after his death they walked outside and rain was splashing against their faces. By the next day, the river had swelled and boats were able to travel.

What would you have said to God, if that had been your child? Was God mocking them? Why should they believe when God seemed so heartless and even cruel? Why would He heal a nobleman's son with a high fever, but not their son inflicted with the same malady?

They went on believing. They learned that faith is not merely receiving from God what we ask, but it is the ability to accept whatever God gives us.

> Though He giveth or He taketh,
> God His children ne'er forsaketh;
> His the loving purpose solely
> To preserve them pure and holy.

Carolina Sandell Berg, 1858; tr. Ernst W. Olson, 1925. Text reprinted by permission of the Board of Publication, Lutheran Church in America.

This couple has long since died and gone to heaven, where they have been reunited with their child. I'm sure that the purposes of God are much clearer to them now than they were back in those days in a jungle in China. Their faith survived intact.

Faith grows when our prayers are answered; it also grows when our prayers are not answered. In either case, we know that Jesus, who is not limited by space, walks with us every step of the way.

For Further Consideration

An Analysis of the Signs and Wonders Movement

"Unless you people see miraculous signs and wonders, . . . you will never believe," Jesus said (John 4:48).

Some people teach that we could evangelize more effectively if we had "signs and wonders" to authenticate the gospel message. In fact, the Vineyard Movement, begun in the 1970s, teaches that our churches should be characterized by healings, along with "words of knowledge" and speaking in tongues. We've all seen people "slain in the spirit," falling down in the presence of television preachers, supposedly under the power of the Holy Spirit. There are also reports of angelic visitations, predictions made about coming revivals, and personal stories claiming virtually any "miracle" one can imagine.

Back in 1995, reports were circulated of a revival dubbed "the Toronto Blessing," telling of experiences that went beyond the accepted "signs and wonders" phenomena. The chairs in the meeting room were stacked to clear the floor so that participants could do "carpet time," falling down in the presence of God. Many barked like dogs or roared like lions, while others laughed uncontrollably, presumably all under the control of the Spirit.

Although the Vineyard Movement withdrew its support from the Toronto Blessing, the two movements share some common themes. First, that signs and wonders should continue in the church today. In short, the evangelical church should shift to a worldview that is more conducive to the supernatural. Second, that gifts such as healing and prophecy can be obtained by observation and learning to "call the Spirit down."

A brief evaluation cannot do justice to this movement, but I do believe that a few comments are in order. I am well aware that many fine Christians with whom we have much in common support this phenomenon. Also, my remarks, though I believe to be fair, are not representative of all within the movement.

THE INFLUENCE OF POP CULTURE

Many of these signs and wonders are more in keeping with the hyper-spirituality of popular culture than the teachings of the Bible. For example, Peter Wagner gives five steps to be followed in obtaining the miracle of healing. In the fourth stage, he says, "sometimes there is a fluttering of the eyelids or a kind of aura that surrounds the person. Sometimes there are other manifestations."[3] One writer says that when this gift is conferred there is a change in the color of the evangelist's hands that proves "you've got some intercession that's gone up that Papa's saying yes to. . . . Because when my hands turn purple it means you're getting through to Royalty; you're getting through to the top."[4]

Evangelists are encouraged to follow the lead of those who "taunt the spirits" in an anticipation of an evening of power. The late John Wimber, who founded the Vineyard Movement, said that the two most important miracles for impressing unbelievers are "falling in the power of the Spirit and filling teeth."[5] Some of the Vineyard prophets actually claim to "smell God" when those seeking healing come to them as the walls of their offices dissolve as they see visions of the person's past. Clouds with dollar signs appear over the heads of people in an auditorium who have financial problems. John Armstrong is quite correct when he writes, "Advance courses in healing are offered, as though it were training in the magical arts."[6]

Such an approach blends nicely with the superstition, magic, and spiritual dimensions of the New Age Movement. There are similarities with the book *A Course in Miracles,* by Helen Schuchman, who says it is possible to access latent powers to perform all kinds of feats that will make your life better. No wonder Wimber actually defended the practice of employing medieval relics in healing. "In the Catholic Church for over a 1,200-year period, people were healed as a result of touching the relics of the saints. We Protestants have difficulty with that . . . but we healers shouldn't, because there is nothing theologically out of line with that."[7]

Alan Cole, who has served Christ in many different cultures, says of the Vineyard Movement:

> None of these signs are new to me (healings, visions, tongues, exorcisms). But the trouble is that I have seen

every one of them (yes, tongues too) in non-Christian religions, and outwardly there was no difference in the signs, except that one was done in the name of Jesus and the other was not. Of course, if the person was also responding to the Gospel, there was real and lasting change in life. That is why I cannot get excited about healings in themselves, and why I can reverently understand how Jesus used them sparingly, and retreated when the crowds became too great.[8]

We must remember that every issue of the *Christian Science Sentinel* contains articles about miraculous healings. Pakistani Muslims claim that one of their revered saints, Baba Farid, has healed people with incurable diseases, and thousands of Hindus claim healings each year at the temple dedicated to Venkatewara in Tirupathi.[9]

In an excellent book, *Blessing the Church?* the authors, who are all charismatics (and thus more sympathetic to the Vineyard/Toronto phenomena), are concerned about the drift they see in their own movement. They concede that the emphasis of the Toronto Blessing has "led to the pernicious practice of using contemporary 'revelation' as the basis for doctrines and the justification for the formulation of new teaching and practice within the church which has no biblical foundation."[10] They lament the fact that so many people ignore Bible doctrine because they claim to receive their messages directly from God.

Recall that the Catholic Church used their practice of miracles against the Protestants during the Reformation, arguing that Mother Church possessed signs and wonders. After Luther published his Ninety-five Theses and the Reformation was underway, the Catholic Church argued that it had statues that would cry and relics that multiplied themselves (thus the explanation for the hundreds of pieces of wood that were supposed to have come from the cross of Christ). Furthermore, Rome argued that it had recorded apparitions of Mary and Christ. Miraculous healings took place when the worshipers touched the relics of the saints. "Where are your miracles?" the Catholic Church taunted the Reformers.

The Reformers insisted that the gospel had its own power. "I am not ashamed of the gospel, because it is the power of God for the salvation of everyone who believes: first for the Jew, then for the Gentile" (Romans 1:16). When Paul came to Corinth, he chided the people who sought signs: "Jews demand miraculous signs and Greeks look for wisdom, but we preach Christ crucified: a stumbling block to Jews and foolishness to Gentiles, but to those whom God has called, both Jews and Greeks, Christ the power of God and the wisdom of God" (1 Corinthians 1:22–24).

We should not be surprised that the members of the Vineyard Fellowship deny that the Scriptures are sufficient for doctrine and the rule of life. Like the mystics of a bygone era, they are interested in what God is saying to them *now*. Often these revelations are compatible with Scripture; at other times these moments of illumination are bizarre and outside of the limits of scriptural sanction. Certainly this would be true of the Toronto Blessing, with its animal noises, laughter, and "carpet time."

SIGNS AND WONDERS IN THE BIBLE

"But," we can already hear the question, "were there not plenty of signs and wonders in the Bible? Why should we think God has limited Himself in this age?" As one person said to me, "If God is the same from age to age, why would His works not continue to our times?"

These are fair questions. So I would like to begin by saying that yes, there might be signs and wonders today, for we have no right to limit God. But our first obligation is to find out the biblical purpose of these phenomena and then judge contemporary claims by this standard. This is not to say that we will know in every instance whether a miracle is a work of God, but the weight of the biblical evidence will give us the confidence to reject some miracles as not being God given and keep us from uncritical acceptance of others. Perhaps here, as nowhere else, it is possible that well-meaning people can be deceived.

In the Bible, the phrase "signs and wonders" refers to redemptive acts of God. "He sent his signs and wonders into your midst, O Egypt, against Pharaoh and all his servants" (Psalm 135:9). Thus we should not be surprised that the New Testament applies the expression to the ministry of Christ (Acts 2:19; 4:30). Those who saw the signs were expected to contemplate these redemptive acts and be led to faith in Christ. Often these miracles were accompanied with related discourses that correlated the miracle with the deeper spiritual truths Jesus wanted us to grasp.[11]

However—and this is important—not all signs and wonders in the Bible are attributed to the gracious acts of God. The Egyptian magicians could match Moses miracle-for-miracle, turning the Nile into blood, producing frogs, and the like. Not until the magicians were expected to bring forth gnats were they forced to admit failure (Exodus 8:18). Interestingly, these false wonders are not interpreted for us in Scripture. We are not told if these magicians did their miracles by sleight of hand or by the power of the devil. All that we know is that these soothsayers "did the same" miracles as Moses (Exodus 7:22).

Second, the Scripture warns that even if a prophet is accurate in predicting the future, this does not prove that he has been sent by God (if he is inaccurate, then we can be sure that he is not of God). Moses said that even if the sign or wonder which he foretells comes to pass, the prophet is to be rejected if he says, "Let us follow other gods" (Deuteronomy 13:2; see also 18:20–22). In other words, the primary test of a true prophet is not the signs and wonders he is able to perform but what he believes. His doctrine takes precedence over his miracles, even if those miracles happen as predicted. The fact that today's miracle workers often belittle doctrine and assert that more doctrinal openness is needed in the church ought to be a clue that not all is well in the Signs and Wonders Movement.

Many false prophets do not use the name of a false god, but ascribe their prophecies to the Lord God Almighty. Hananiah, who claimed to have a message from God, was so persuasive that even the prophet Jeremiah believed his predictions! Yet Hananiah turned out to be a false prophet and was judged by God (Jeremiah 28). To put it clearly: Not all miracles are from God, nor is every prediction that comes to pass proof that God has spoken. This does not mean that God-given miracles do not take place today, but we are deluded if we think that everyone who does miracles in the name of Jesus is from God.

In the previous chapter, I alluded to the words of Jesus, "Not everyone who says to me, 'Lord, Lord,' will enter the kingdom of heaven, but only he who does the will of my Father who is in heaven. Many will say to me on that day, 'Lord, Lord, did we not prophesy in your name, and in your name drive out demons and perform many miracles?' Then I will tell them plainly, 'I never knew you. Away from me, you evildoers!'" (Matthew 7:21–23). We have no reason to believe that these miracles and exorcisms didn't happen; Jesus did not question that. These people believed that their entrance into heaven was assured, given their miraculous powers and faithful service. No wonder Jesus predicted that false Christs would "deceive the elect—if that were possible" (Mark 13:22). As Carson says, "That means it will take more than the usual discernment to see what is askew; and our generation of believers is not noteworthy for discernment."[12]

Third, even the signs and wonders recorded in Scripture were insufficient to persuade the unconverted to believe in Christ. The more miracles He performed, the more opposition toward Him grew. On the day of Pentecost, Peter said that Christ was "accredited by God to you by miracles, wonders and signs" (Acts 2:22); yet most in the crowd were not brought to faith until they heard the gospel through Peter's lips.

Perhaps we could summarize it this way: Miracles attested to the person of Christ for those who were open to the truth; even those who had their doubts (as did Thomas) were reassured by the miraculous. But the skeptics either denied the miracles or ascribed them to the devil. This best explains why Jesus performed miracles so that some would believe but, on the other hand, refused to do miracles for the truly skeptical. Even today there is no compelling evidence that when the unconverted see miracles they are more disposed to believe the gospel.

Interestingly, no church in the New Testament is chided for not doing more signs and wonders. But Paul rebuked churches for an unclear gospel (Galatians), an overemphasis on gifts along with a worldly spirit (Corinthians), and the dangers of accepting a gnostic view of Christ (Colossians). Christ's rebukes to the seven churches addressed in the book of Revelation were either doctrinal, moral, or both. Never once did He hint that they needed more signs and wonders.

All this is not to say that authentic signs and wonders cannot occur today, or even that they do not occur today. There is no hard scriptural evidence that the gift of miracles has been rescinded. What we do know is that such miracles are of lesser importance than a clear gospel witness and the quest for holiness. Yes, we can believe God today for miracles, but we cannot demand them; and we should not be led to expect them on a regular basis. And we most assuredly cannot ascribe to the modern notion that they are needed to do effective evangelism in a culture already saturated with bogus miracles of every sort.

We can do no better than quote the words of Jesus, "A wicked and adulterous generation asks for a miraculous sign! But none will be given it except the sign of the prophet Jonah. For as Jonah was three days and three nights in the belly of a huge fish, so the Son of Man will be three days and three nights in the heart of the earth" (Matthew 12:39–40). Today, multitudes thirst for signs but will not believe the powerful evidence for the death and resurrection of Christ.

The question of whether there is "healing in the atonement" or whether the gift of healing should still be practiced today will be considered in a subsequent chapter. For now, we turn our attention to another miracle that should convince us.

NOTES

1. Warren W. Wiersbe, *The Bible Exposition Commentary* (Wheaton: Scripture Press, 1992), 303.

2. J. C. Macaulay, *Expository Commentary on John,* 2d ed. (Chicago: Moody, 1978), 61.

3. John H. Armstrong, "In Search of Spiritual Power," in Michael Scott Horton, ed., *Power Religion: The Selling Out of the Evangelical Church?* (Chicago: Moody, 1992), 74.

4. Ibid., 75.

5. Ibid., 76.

6. Ibid.

7. Ibid., 77.

8. Quoted by D. A. Carson, "The Purpose of Signs and Wonders in the New Testament," in *Power Religion,* 95.

9. Ibid.

10. Clifford Hill, Peter Fenwick, David Forbes, and David Noakes, *Blessing the Church?* (Surrey, England:: Inter Publishing Service, Eagle, 1995), 4.

11. Carson, "The Purpose of Signs and Wonders," 93.

12. Ibid.

Chapter Three

Jesus, Lord of Our Impossibilities

There is no doubt that God calls us to do the impossible.

Try this.

"Hate what is evil; cling to what is good" (Romans 12:9).

"Love your enemies, do good to those who hate you" (Luke 6:27).

"Be holy, for I am holy" (Leviticus 11:45 KJV).

Such are legitimate commands; all are impossible for us to keep.

One day, Jesus asked a lame man to do the impossible. "Pick up your mat and walk!" The lame man could not believe his ears!

Jesus went to Jerusalem for a feast and stopped at the pool of Bethesda, which [was] surrounded by five covered colonnades. Here a great number of disabled people used to lie—the blind, the lame, the paralyzed. One who was there had been an invalid for thirty-eight years. When Jesus saw him lying there and learned that he had been in this condition for a long time, he asked him, "Do you want to get well?"

"Sir," the invalid replied, "I have no one to help me into the pool when the water is stirred. While I am trying to get in, someone else goes down ahead of me."

Then Jesus said to him, "Get up! Pick up your mat and walk." At once the man was cured; he picked up his mat and walked. (John 5:2–9)

This pool has been excavated and can be seen today within the walls on the eastern side of the Old City of Jerusalem. It is near the Sheep Gate, or today's "Saint Stephen's Gate," named for the first martyr, who was stoned nearby. The pool itself was called *Bethesda,* meaning "house of mercy," but this place was anything but a house of mercy.

Picture the crowd of disabled folks lounging near the pool. All of them wanted healing; all of them hoped for a miracle. Jesus, with infinite power at His disposal, could have healed them all but focused on one man, a "certain man" (v. 5 KJV), who had been an invalid for thirty-eight years. This is proof that God does not treat all men alike. He does not heal all that He could heal; just as He does not save all He could save.

"Do you want to get well?" Jesus asked.

The man does not give a direct answer. Curiously, he replies that he does not have someone to put him into the pool "when the water is stirred." How are we to understand this strange reply? Were others actually healed if they were the first to enter after ripples were seen in the water? And why would this man, having been here for so long, never get into the pool in time to be healed?

Of course, those who read the early version of John's gospel would have had the same questions. In order that readers might be able to account for this "stirring of the water," I believe an ancient scribe added these words, "From time to time an angel of the Lord would come down and stir up the waters. The first one into the pool after each such disturbance would be cured of whatever disease he had" (v. 4, margin).

Some translations insert these words in order to give an explanation for the stirring of the water. But we are not sure that such a stirring actually took place. If people were healed thereby, why would there be such a large number of disabled people at the pool? Or, if the angel came only occasionally, why not more often? It is more likely that no angel came and no one was healed. In those days, as in ours, angels were often thought to be active in the small occurrences of life, even creating a ripple of water in a pool. Apparently the man believed a legend.

Understandably, Jesus ignores his comment.

"Get up!"

Jesus is speaking. "Pick up your mat and walk."

The healings of Christ do not fit a neat pattern. In one instance, the friends of an invalid opened the roof of a hut to let him down in the presence of Jesus (Mark 2:1–5). He appears to have been healed because of the faith of his friends. At other times, Jesus demanded faith on the part of the one who needed the healing (Matthew

9:27–31). Here He simply commanded a man to be healed, not because the man believed, but because of His sovereign will.

The man was not expected to have any prior faith (though obeying Jesus' command was a sign of *immediate* faith). Incredibly, as the story unfolds we learn that he does not even know the name of the One who healed him. This was one of those sovereign miracles. Some are blessed more than others and often for no discernable reason.

From the group, Jesus selects a man, one particular man, who had been lame for thirty-eight years. And it is to him that He shows His power.

REQUIREMENTS FOR IMPOSSIBLE LIVING

How did Christ help this man do the impossible? And what is the relevance of this miracle for us today?

To Do the Impossible

"Do you want to get well?" That might seem like a foolish question. Of course the man would want to get well!

Perhaps yes; perhaps no.

Don't assume that people want to get well; some would prefer to live with their disability because the thought of having to work for a living is frightening. This man made a living begging; if he were healed he would have to lay aside his beggar's cup, rise early in the morning, and return late in the evening, weary with the demands of a new vocation. He was not trained for any particular line of work, and he would not even know where to begin to earn a few denarii.

The man had become accustomed to being pitied. He had attracted the attention of those who cared, those who gladly offered a helping hand. Now he would have to go it alone. If their disability is manageable, some people might turn down the offer of a divine touch.

The same hesitancy applies to spiritual healing. The alcoholic fears what life might be like without his precious bottle. The glutton fears that diet restrictions might limit the one solitary pleasure he enjoys in his lonely world. And the sensual person, the man who feeds his fleshly desire with pornography or immorality, can't bear the thought of living without those hidden pleasures.

"Do you want to be free?" Jesus asks. They are not sure.

I've met people who admitted they did not want to give up their bitterness because they thought that in doing so they would have to surrender justice. They received grim satisfaction nursing their anger and hoping for revenge. The same can be said for the greedy and the violent. Leaving one behavioral rut for another can be threatening. Not until they are desperate do they cry out for a miracle.

"Sir . . . I have no one to help me into the pool when the water is stirred," the man explained (v. 7). But the fact that he had been at the pool so long, waiting so patiently for a ripple in the water, was proof enough that he actually desired healing. His desire is what counted.

So I ask you, my friend:

Do you wish to be comforted?

Do you wish to be forgiven?

Do you wish to be free from sin's power?

Do you wish to be saved?

God often brings us to the point of weariness with

our sins and excuses. He wants us to become desperate for His intervention. He wants us to "bottom out," willing to have His blessing at any cost. After we have crossed the line and said, "Yes, Lord," we wonder why we did not let Him change us sooner.

Jesus did not always demand faith; but He did demand compliance. He would not have healed this man against his will. So He commanded him, "Get up! Pick up your mat and walk!" The man could have thought he had misunderstood.

How could an invalid do what he by definition *could not* do?

We Must Obey the Impossible

"Get up! Pick up your mat and walk."

The man might have replied, "Cure me, and I will walk!" But Christ reversed it and said, "*Walk* and you shall be cured." The power, of course, was not in the invalid, but in the command.

"Get up!" You will have a new means of transportation.

"Pick up your mat!" You will have a new vocation.

"Walk!" You will have a new future.

As he made the effort to stand, strength entered his body. To his surprise, and to the amazement of those around him, he walked. He walked directly to the temple, most probably to give thanks to God for an unexpected miracle. What a difference between his gloomy morning and his ecstatic evening! Just think of what Jesus can do!

Today we also hear impossible commands: We are to love our enemies, forgive those who have wronged us, and abstain from the appearance of evil. Our problem is that we know what to do, but we don't have the strength to do it. Walter Brueggemann spoke for all of us when he said, "I have found myself discovering that mostly I do not need more advice, but strength. I do not need new information, but the courage, freedom and authorization to act on what I already have been given in the gospel."[1]

One day en route to Jerusalem, Jesus met ten lepers. As required by Old Testament law, "they stood at a distance and called out in a loud voice, 'Jesus, Master, have pity on us!'" (Luke 17:12–13). Jesus gave a command that was possible for them to obey physically, but quite frankly it made no sense. He said, "Go, show yourselves to the priests" (v. 14).

The law required that a healed leper was to go to the priest for verification. The priest would then give him a "clean bill of health" if an inspection proved the man's claims. But it made no sense to trek to a priest if, in fact, the leprosy was obvious. If Jesus had healed these men, they would have reason to seek out the services of a priest, but as it was, their bodies were still afflicted with this dreaded disease.

And yet we read, "And as they went, they were cleansed" (v. 14). When they set out to obey Christ's word, the blotches were still on their skin. But as they walked in sheer faith, their skin became like that of a child. *When Christ commands the impossible, He supplies what He commands.* Paul prayed that we would be faithful until the appearing of Christ, then added, "The one who calls you is faithful and he will do it" (1 Thessalonians 5:24). God works through our wills to overcome our resistance. He gives us commands He knows we cannot keep, but He gives us the grace to do them. And, thankfully, Jesus meets our ultimate obligations for us.

If you think you do not have the power to be reconciled to the person who has wronged you, you are denying Jesus' power. Looked at through your eyes, the command is impossible; looked at through the eyes of Jesus, you can do it. You can say, "God did it through me." We are asked to scale mountains, but when we begin the journey, Jesus walks with us to navigate the difficult terrain. We *can* do what we *should* do.

As for unbelievers, they are commanded to obey, to submit, and to repent. But they lack the ability to do so, unless God sovereignly chooses to work in their lives to effect the gift of salvation. Just like this man at the pool, they cannot walk unless healed by God. Obviously, a further discussion of this is beyond the scope of this chapter.

As for those who do believe, power is given to grow in both obedience and faith. Of course, this strength cannot be taken for granted but must be nourished through the disciplines of the Christian life. Such obedience is not easy; it is often a struggle that in some sense approaches the agony of Christ in Gethsemane. But it can be done.

We Must Persist in the Impossible

This miracle happened on the Sabbath day, and the Jews criticized the man for carrying his mat; after all, that was work and no work was to be done on the Sabbath. "The law forbids you to carry your mat," they said (John 5:10). But we should not think that Jesus asked the man to break the Old Testament Sabbath regulations.

The law forbade the people to carry those products

related to their customary employment on the Sabbath, but carrying this mat was hardly work in the usual sense of the word. It would have been different if the healed man had formed a "mat-carrying company." A lone man carrying his own mat was not breaking the Sabbath.

As the man tested the strength of his new legs, he had a ready answer for his critics. "The man who made me well said to me, 'Pick up your mat and walk'" (v. 11). That would have ended the matter for him, but not for them. They asked who had made him well. For these critics, the person who healed on the Sabbath was more blameworthy than the healed man who carried his mat.

Surprisingly we read, "The man who was healed had no idea who it was, for Jesus had slipped away into the crowd that was there" (v. 13). Imagine! Healed by a divine word, yet ignorant of who spoke it! This is proof that the miracle was one of sovereign grace! Jesus just picked him out of the crowd for a divine encounter.

"Later Jesus found him at the temple and said to him, 'See, you are well again. Stop sinning or something worse may happen to you'" (v. 14). Why was he told to stop sinning? Was his disability really his own fault? *Something worse* could come upon him! What could be worse than suffering from a disability for thirty-eight years?

Let's ponder the text for an explanation.

First, apparently this man's illness was because of a specific sin. This does not mean that everyone who commits a particular sin will be sick, handicapped, or die, but that some instances of suffering are because of an individual sin. We do not know what this sin was, but in some way it contributed to his condition. Elsewhere, illness and death are specifically not tied to specific sins (see John 9:1–3).

There is only one thing that could be worse than being an invalid for thirty-eight years, and that is a final judgment, the condemnation that leads to hell's fire. There is something worse than earthly suffering, and that is falling under the heavy hand of the wrath of God.

Jesus' words lead me to conclude that this man was not a believer in Jesus at the time of the miracle. This is confirmed by the fact that he did not even know who healed him, or who Christ was. So when Jesus said, "Stop sinning," this was, in effect, the same as commanding this man to repent. And I believe he did.

"The man went away and told the Jews that it was Jesus who had made him well" (v. 15). He announced to all who would listen that Jesus was able to heal simply by His divine word. The impossible became possible in the presence of the Lord of Glory.

Just as Jesus chose a man to be healed, so He chooses those who are to be saved. A few paragraphs after this incident we read, "For just as the Father raises the dead and gives them life, even so the Son gives life to whom he is pleased to give it" (v. 21). When we were crippled, spiritually speaking; when we were in sin and without Christ, He came to us and saved us. Thanks to His gracious prerogative and His undeserved mercy.

Some scholars have seen a similarity between this man and the impotent nation of Israel (Deuteronomy 2:14). Both were in the wilderness for thirty-eight years; both were pictures of tragedy. Yet, Jesus *saw* him, Jesus *knew* him, and Jesus *spoke* to him. Jesus appears to have come to the pool just to meet him. Here we see the predestinating power of God. This man, who apparently had no friends, was helpless, but he was also hopeless. Then Jesus came.

Can we do the impossible? No, we can only do what is possible, but God can do the impossible. Even our obedience is His gracious gift. The bottom line: When God asks us to do the impossible, the power is in the command. He can do in us "that which is well-pleasing in his sight" (Hebrews 13:21 KJV).

This miracle attracted a wider audience. "So, because Jesus was doing these things on the Sabbath, the Jews persecuted him" (John 5:16). Jesus gave an explanation as to who He was. "My Father is always at his work to this very day, and I, too, am working" (v. 17).

The Jews knew exactly what He meant. They affirmed that He was calling God His Father, and therefore "making himself equal with God" (v. 18).

This miracle is another powerful confirmation that Jesus is indeed, the Messiah of Israel and the Savior of the world. He who spoke to a lame man and commanded him to walk has spoken to us, and with His command has come the power to obey. And in the future He shall command our bodies to rise from the dead, and they shall obey.

> I tell you the truth, a time is coming and has now come when the dead will hear the voice of the Son of God and those who hear will live. For as the Father has life in himself, so he has granted the Son to have life in himself. And he has given him authority to judge because he is the Son of Man. (vv. 25–27)

This miracle is another reason to believe.

ᐯor Further Consideration

The Role of Angels in Today's Spiritual Culture

"From time to time an angel of the Lord would come down and stir up the waters" (John 5:4, margin). That was the popular explanation for the moving water, possibly a small whirlpool that occasionally bubbled up in the pool of Bethesda. The people, bless them, had put their faith in a legend, a myth that could not heal them. I have no doubt that an angel could stir a pool of water, but it is unlikely that God gives them such assignments.

What do we make of the growing number of "angel stories" told and retold every day? As of this writing, Hollywood has produced more than three dozen films, made-for-TV movies, and series featuring heavenly beings. Roger Ebert, a film critic not noted for his commitment to the Bible, wrote, "These scenarios are all wrong, wrong, wrong from a theological point of view (which is the only one worth having about angels). All the authorities agree that God created angels before the beginning—before there was earth or sea or sky, or men and women."[2] *Say it again, Roger!*

We do not expect theological accuracy from Hollywood; indeed, sometimes even respect and decency are lacking. Thus, in the movie *Michael,* John Travolta portrays the biblical archangel as a slob; a brawling, promiscuous, but supposedly lovable slob. Covering his wings with an old trench coat, Michael joins three tabloid journalists on a journey to Chicago. Along the way he seduces women and he spends a night in jail.

Obviously, this scenario is much more akin to the fallen angel, Lucifer, than it is to Michael, the archangel, the "prince who protects" the children of Israel (Daniel 12:1) and who fought with the devil over the body of Moses (Jude 9). Hollywood has it wrong, *very* wrong.

My concern is not with such gross distortions of angels, however. Something much more sinister is taking place with this new angel fad, something that might be more damaging than trash television or blatant, liberal theology. I refer to this: that millions of evangelicals are accepting the notion that angels are about us, waiting to help anyone who is in distress, regardless of his or her religious convictions.

The basic formula of the *Touched by an Angel* TV program, as stated by the producers, is this: "The angel meets her assigned human at a crossroads in his or her life. The angel (by the power of God) performs a miracle to bring that person to a point of decision or revelation. He or she, by their own free will, then takes life-changing action."[3]

Thus, in virtually every episode, a troubled person is helped; perhaps there is a physical healing or an emotional barrier is overcome. Sometimes the needy person might be facing a personal crisis in his or her marriage or with the children. Whatever, an angel is used by God to resolve the crisis, proving that there is a spiritual dimension to the world and that the Almighty stands ready to help us by sending angels to those who least deserve or expect it. Each show has a "feel good" ending, since a crisis has been resolved and the troubled person has turned a corner, setting out in a new direction.

Why do I object to this harmless story line?

These stories are loaded with theology, a cultural theology that reinforces prevalent views about man and God. Through its pleasing portrayals of needy people, helped by heavenly messengers, these notions lob a grenade at the heart of the Christian gospel.

Let me explain why popular cultural views about angels are contrary to what the Bible teaches.

A FALSE VIEW OF HUMAN NATURE

First, this angel theology assumes that people are basically good, rather than sinners who stand in desperate need of God's saving grace. The show avoids concepts such as sin and the total depravity of the human race. Everyone has goodness within, waiting for it to be unleashed. Indeed, one of the show's actors says "there might be an angel in everyone of us, waiting to do a miracle"[4]

This reinforces the prevailing myth that sin is not our problem; rather, we must simply overcome a feeling of disconnectedness, a need to know how God's help can be enlisted. Thankfully, an angel comes to help in a crisis, and there is relief in knowing that at last one has made contact with God.

Biblically, an understanding of our sinfulness is central to our understanding of how we must approach God. If we don't know how bad off we are in the presence of a holy God, we will try to access Him in ways He despises. Thus a wrong view of man always leads to a wrong view of God.

Again, let me explain.

A FALSE VIEW OF GOD

Like Cain, who thought God could be approached in any creative way, popular culture teaches that ordinary people, if they have enough ordinary goodwill, can have contact with God without a mediator, without a sacrifice, and without blood.

Shows like *Touched by an Angel* have no place for Christ; neither His cross nor His resurrection is necessary for us to make contact with the "powers that be." Angels are waiting to help us get connected. They are more approachable than God; thus, it is possible to be in touch with the spiritual world without facing the more difficult task of knowing how to appease God.

"But," you protest, "it does not claim to be a Christian program but is committed to presenting a generic faith, showing that there are people who believe in God and that angels are real beings, just as the Bible says." But the point cannot be made too strongly that these assumptions reinforce a destructive cultural stereotype.

What do we make of the angel stories—the reports of angels intervening to help people? Before we answer that question, we have to cover an important bit of biblical data to put matters into perspective.

ANGELS AND MORE ANGELS

All angels were created good, but some joined in Lucifer's rebellion and became evil angels. Both good and evil angels are independent creatures, not recycled dead people, as Hollywood often portrays them to be. They do not earn their wings by good behavior.

We must affirm that there is a great deal of similarity between the evil angels and the "elect" angels, as Paul calls them (1 Timothy 5:21). Satan is presented in the Bible as having a keen intellect, a full complement of emotions, and a will by which he rebelled against God. Although at one time he stood in God's presence, orchestrating the praise of the entire angelic host, he chose his own path in the cosmos. As a result, he is on a forced march to destruction, en route to his final destination of torment and humiliation in hell.

Unfortunately, he did not fall alone, but took a percentage of the angelic host with him (perhaps one third, according to Revelation 12:4). At any rate, he has a multitude of helpers who do his bidding and seek to extend his kingdom. These helpers are known in Scripture as demons.

When Jesus was on earth, Satan mustered all of his powers to try to divert the Son of God from His calling. He tried to kill the Christ Child when Herod slaughtered all boys under two years of age in the environs of Bethlehem (Matthew 2:16). Since the plan failed, he tried to get Christ to sin in the desert (Matthew 4:1–11); later, he continued his opposition, but Christ decisively defeated him on the cross.

Satan was unsuccessful, of course. Facing the cross, Christ said, "Now is the time for judgment on this world; now the prince of this world will be driven out" (John 12:31).

THE SIMILARITY BETWEEN GOOD AND BAD ANGELS

We can't always tell the difference between good and bad angels. The evil angels are willing to make as many concessions as possible to deceive the unwary. The angels of darkness turn themselves into angels of light so that people will be confused about their real identity (see 2 Corinthians 11:14).

1. *Evil angels are willing to mouth solid, evangelical doctrine.* When Christ was in the synagogue in Capernaum, He met a man with an unclean spirit who, when confronted by Christ, cried out, "What do you want with us, Jesus of Nazareth? Have you come to destroy us? I know who you are—the Holy One of God!" (Mark 1:24).

What is more, demons confessed that Christ was the Son of God. "What do you want with me, Jesus, Son of the Most High God? Swear to God that you won't torture me!" (Mark 5:7). These are the words of a demon responding to Christ's command to leave the demented man. These demons could, in effect, sign an evangelical statement of faith that affirmed that Christ was "The Holy One of God," or "The Son of the Most High God."

Of course, demons do not make such admissions willingly or gladly. But when in the presence of Christ, or when attempting to deceive, they will confess correct doctrine. Yes, they are capable of appearing and quoting, "Hear O Israel: The Lord our God, the Lord is one" (Deuteronomy 6:4), if the words will deceive one of their victims.

2. *Evil angels will, if possible, duplicate the miracles of Christ.* Paul warned that Satan would come with "counterfeit miracles, signs and wonders" (2 Thessalonians 2:9). Evil angels will do helpful miracles if they can and if it serves their long-term goals, namely, diverting people from the purity of the gospel of Christ.

A man who was healed from a serious disease in a so-called healing meeting discovered that he inherited "demonic darkness," that is, a persistent sense that he now had an evil presence near him. When he rebuked Satan, the emotional and spiritual cloud left him but his disease returned. We should not be surprised that healings occur in all the religions of the world. Satan is willing to give something that appears good, in exchange for blind allegiance.

3. *Evil angels use "super-apostles" who present themselves as experts in spirituality.* These persons convincingly lead people to believe that all people have within themselves the power to find God, that they can have direct contact with God by following the right *techniques.*

These apostles invite people to come to God "just as they are," not to be cleansed and forgiven but to be accepted on the basis of their own merit as humans. They are to come to receive the help they deserve. "Come one, come all" and "come in your own way." And so we come once again to the grand lie: *Anyone can make contact with God without a mediator, without a God-appointed sacrifice, and without blood.*

Thus it is not possible for us to always distinguish the good from the bad. It is simply not wise to navigate the metaphysical landscape without a map, a guide that lets us call these angelic beings by their correct designation.

TELLING THE DIFFERENCE

So the question is: How do we interpret the dramatic rescues, the healings, and the help given to people who are in desperate straits? What do we say about the accounts of "divine intervention" of heavenly beings that make everything turn out just right, regardless of what people believe about Christ? Think through the following:

1. *God's good angels are given assignments limited to the people of God.* They are not sent indiscriminately to all men and women. "Are not all angels ministering spirits sent to serve those who will inherit salvation?" (Hebrews 1:14). Thus we have the function of angels defined for us in Scripture. If angels are ever sent to help those who have not accepted Christ and therefore will not "inherit salvation" (Hebrews 1:14), we have no account of it in Scripture.

2. *God's good angels participate in acts of judgment for the unconverted.* Yes, angels are sometimes sent to the unconverted, but only to judge them. We think immediately of the angels that visited with Abraham and had the responsibility of executing judgment on Sodom and Gomorrah. Angels did help Lot escape the city, but only because he was a believer in Jehovah and therefore a "righteous man" (2 Peter 2:7).

Repeatedly in the book of Revelation angels are directly involved in executing judgment on those who have not come under the protection of Christ's sacrifice. For example, in chapter 14 a succession of angels comes announcing judgment. One warns that if anyone worships the beast, "he, too, will drink of the wine of God's fury, which has been poured full strength into the cup of his wrath. He will be tormented with burning sulfur in the presence of the holy angels and of the Lamb" (Revelation 14:10). The angel that followed announced the impending judgment and the next angel executed it.

Read carefully: "Still another angel, who had charge of the fire, came from the altar and called in a loud voice to him who had the sharp sickle, 'Take your sharp sickle and gather the clusters of grapes from the earth's vine, because its grapes are ripe'" (v. 18). Then notice what this angel does.

"The angel swung his sickle on the earth, gathered its grapes and threw them into the great winepress of God's wrath" (v. 19). Later in the book, an angel invites the birds in midheaven to "eat the flesh of kings, generals, and mighty men" (19:17–18), now that God has destroyed them in judgment.

Needless to say, *Touched by an Angel* does not feature angels coming to execute the wicked. These Hollywood angels are always doing good deeds, even for people who might not be particularly religious—even for people who think of Christ as a teacher, not the Savior.

3. *Evil angels have all of the essential powers of good angels.* As far as we know, evil angels can perform many assignments for Satan that are similar to those done by God's angels. Think of the awesome "victory" (albeit temporary) Satan wins when millions of people mistake his intervention as the intervention of God and His angels!

Remember, Satan's goal is not to create as much misery as he can on planet earth; he wants to make us comfortable while keeping his eventual goals in sight. His primary objective is to spread false doctrine, to reinforce the cultural conception of God. He wants people to believe in a benevolent God who dispenses help to all. It is naive to say, as some do, that reported miracles must be the work of good angels because the effects are good and beneficial. We must boldly say that "good" miracles can be done by "bad" angels.

Unless spirituality is based on the authority of the Bible, it will always spawn superstitions and a gullible generation. We've all heard of Elvis sightings; and now that Princess Diana has become an international icon, I've heard that there are sightings of her too. The famous spiritist Emanuel Swedenborg recognized the difficulty of distinguishing good angels and bad. After years of spiritism, he wrote,

> When spirits begin to speak with a man, he ought to beware that he believes nothing whatever from them; for they say almost anything . . . they would tell so many lies, and indeed with solemn affirmation, that a man would be astonished . . . if a man listens and believes, they press on and deceive, and seduce in [many] ways.[5]

The fear that Paul had for the saints in Corinth should be ours today: "But I am afraid that just as Eve was deceived by the serpent's cunning, your minds may somehow be led astray from your sincere and pure devotion to Christ" (2 Corinthians 11:3).

Elsewhere he warned, "But even if we or an angel from heaven should preach a gospel other than the one we have preached to you, let him be eternally condemned!" (Galatians 1:8). Angels are not reliable as a source of revelation simply because we might be listening to the wrong ones!

NOTES

1. Quoted in Warren W. Wiersbe, *Preaching and Teaching with Imagination*, (Wheaton, Ill.: Scripture Press, Victor Books, 1994), 64.

2. Roger Ebert, quoted in *Citizen*, December 1997.

3. Ibid., 7.

4. Ibid.

5. Emanuel Swedenborg, quoted in John Ankerberg and John Weldon, *The Facts on Channeling* (Chattanooga: John Ankerberg Evangelistic Association, 1988), 8.

Chapter Four

Jesus, Lord of Our Daily Bread

What a difference Jesus can make!

Bring your camera as we tour the shores of Galilee, where Jesus performed another miracle that proves why He alone is a qualified Savior. This is the only miracle recorded in all four Gospels. And it introduces us to some of the most satisfying spiritual truths we will ever encounter. So deep, so profound, that many who read His words will not believe them.

Jesus used hunger, bread, and the subject of nutrition to help us understand the yearnings within our "inner self." In fact, He teaches us that our souls are more important than our bodies and warns us of the danger of being satisfied with synthetic spiritual foods that give the illusion of fulfillment. In an age with a blizzard of religious options, we must return to the One who claims to be the only source of nourishment and strength.

Jesus teaches us that there are two kinds of food. Physical food is necessary for the body, and spiritual food is necessary for the soul. Even as children we exasperated our parents if we missed so much as a single meal. Just so, as we grow older, a spiritual hunger arises within, and if it is misdirected, we will search for inner peace and meaning in all the wrong places. In our day there is a smorgasbord of options, all attractively packaged, all with a mixture of sugar and poison.

Jesus will help us. We will not only see Him as the Bread of Life, but also better understand why He alone can satisfy our spiritual yearnings. There is a perfect match between our appetite and the meal to which He invites us.

CAPTURING THE SCENE
ONE SNAPSHOT AT A TIME

If you visit Israel today, tour guides will show you the hill along the sea of Galilee believed to be the spot where this miracle was performed. Let's travel there in our imaginations, seeing the sights and hearing the sounds.

The Multitude

A restless and hungry crowd gathered to find Jesus, the Great Miracle Worker, as He came to the shores of Galilee. "Some time after this, Jesus crossed to the far shore of the Sea of Galilee (that is, the Sea of Tiberias), and a great crowd of people followed him because they saw the miraculous signs he had performed on the sick" (John 6:1–2).

Five thousand men, along with half as many women and children, swelled the crowd to perhaps seven or eight thousand. The people were weary, complaining, and confused. There was no central public address system, nor were there ice cream vendors or toilets.

"When Jesus looked up and saw a great crowd coming toward him, he said to Philip, 'Where shall we buy bread for these people to eat?' He asked this only to test him, for he already had in mind what he was going to do" (vv. 5–6). This was no emergency; no need to be anxious about the great challenge that surrounded them. His plans were laid, the future was known, and the results assured. For the disciples, it was a test; for Jesus, it was just one more day of obedience to the Father.

The disciples had three options. Their initial response, according to the account in Mark, was to say, "Send the people away so they can go to the surrounding countryside and villages and buy themselves something to eat" (Mark 6:36). They were not hardhearted, just realistic. What were they to do? Like us watching refugees on television, they felt both compassion and helplessness; a willingness to do something, along with the futility of knowing that nothing (or very little) could be done.

Jesus will have none of it: "*You* give them something to eat," He replies (Mark 6:37, italics added). In the presence of a sovereign God, His people are commanded to do what they cannot. How can they do what only God can do? Again, the power would be in Jesus' command.

The disciples suggest a second possibility: take an offering, find out how much money could be collected among themselves and possibly other contributors, and see what might be done. "Philip answered him, 'Eight months' wages would not buy enough bread for each one to have a bite!" (John 6:7). A quick estimate of the amount of available money was some two hundred denarii (one denarius was an average day's wage). But Philip was quite right. This amount of money would not be enough for everyone to have "a bite." Nor a few crumbs.

A third possibility was to expect Jesus to do something. "Andrew, Simon Peter's brother, spoke up, 'Here is a boy with five small barley loaves and two small fish, but how far will they go among so many?'" (vv. 8–9). Like many of us, Andrew displayed both faith and doubt. Yes, this boy's lunch could be multiplied; but by itself it was woefully inadequate.

We are struck by the great need in comparison to the meager supply. We should pause to remind ourselves just how far this boy's lunch would go on its own. Perhaps crumbs for a few; nothing for the rest of the estimated crowd of five thousand plus. We can almost hear the despair in Andrew's voice, "But how far will they go among so many?"

Behind his question is a hint of faith, the suspicion that Jesus might do something extraordinary. The fact that Andrew brought the boy to Jesus is proof enough that he believed a miracle was possible. If His Master could turn water into wine and heal a boy at a distance of twenty miles, anything was possible. Maybe Jesus would turn a boy's lunch into a banquet.

Jesus chose to use this unknown boy. He would use the lunch of a lad whose name does not appear in the pages of Scripture. But Jesus knew who the boy was, and He knew where Andrew was. We do not need to send

Jesus our address; we do not need to wave a flag so He can see us in a crowd. We do not need to introduce ourselves to Him. Luther said regarding those who are called by God, "When He hath need of thee, He will know where to find thee." So the wise and sovereign God chose to put Andrew and the boy together that both might be at the behest of Jesus.

We must never despise the day of small things. The crowds might hold us in contempt; our friends might misunderstand us; but we must never underestimate what God can do with a boy and his lunch. It's not just that Jesus used a boy. Barley loaves were common among the poor, and fish were plentiful. He used a *poor* boy for a miracle.

We don't know whether the boy needed to be coaxed. If he was hesitant, we would understand; you don't give your lunch to a stranger. But as it turned out, giving what he had to Jesus was best, not just for the crowd, but also for him. If he had kept the food in his knapsack, he would have had a full stomach and that would have been the end of the story. By giving it to Jesus, he had his full stomach, and so did thousands of others! And he probably got his share of the twelve baskets gathered after the meal was over.

On one level we can say that the miracle was not dependent on the boy's lunch. The Creator did not find it "easier" to create the food now that He had a bit of food in His hands. But Jesus seldom works without us; He does not bypass His people in doing His work. He can save the lost without our witness; He can build His church without our cooperation. And He can feed the hungry without our lunch.

What we have in our hands is ours and can only do what it can do; but when it is transferred into Christ's hands, there is no guessing as to what it might do. That which is in our hands we lose; what is in Christ's hands, we keep. And it will be ours for all of eternity. To put it differently, what is in our hands is nothing; what is in Jesus' hands is everything. Let us take what we have and put it in contact with Omnipotence.

The great crowd gathered because they had seen the "miraculous signs" Jesus had just done. We could argue that they were following Jesus for the wrong reason, to see if they could benefit from His power and authority. Miracle workers never lack for an audience.

But at least for now, Jesus did not chide them for their wrong motives. He saw the crowd before Him; He felt their hunger and chose to do something about it. And He knew that in the process some would have their spiritual needs revealed. Some would accept Him as the Bread from heaven and others would not, but the invitation would be given to all.

Small lunch, big miracle.

Perhaps D. L. Moody is one of the best examples of a person who had little to give Jesus, but nevertheless put what he had into the Lord's hands. He was so poorly educated that when reading the Bible aloud, if he came to a word he could not pronounce (and I'm told it happened often), he would stop, make a comment, and then continue reading on the other side of the word! His grammar was atrocious and his personal style irksome. But through his ministry thousands were converted, schools were begun, and both Great Britain and the

United States were spiritually revived. He was just another boy who gave his lunch to Jesus.

We see the crowd. We see the need. And we see a boy. What we still haven't seen is the big miracle. But now we focus our camera and see it happen before our eyes.

The Miracle

"Jesus said, 'Have the people sit down.' There was plenty of grass in that place, and the men sat down, about five thousand of them. Jesus then took the loaves, gave thanks, and distributed to those who were seated as much as they wanted. He did the same with the fish" (John 6:10–11). Mark tells us explicitly that Jesus gave the bread to the disciples, who acted like ushers by giving the bread to the crowd.

I can't prove it, but I believe the miracle took place in the hands of Jesus. The disciples could only give away what they had received; only Jesus could keep giving beyond what He had in his hands. Imagine! Peter came to Jesus for a bit of fish; he was amazed that there was enough for him and for others too. Each disciple came to Jesus, and each came away with enough food for dozens of people sitting on the ground. And no matter how often the disciples returned, their arms were always full if they came expecting to receive what He had waiting for them. The people received "as much as they wanted" (v. 11). And if there had been twenty thousand on the hillside, they too would have been fed. A big miracle is no more difficult for Deity than a small one. Omnipotence has an unending supply. What a picnic!

When everyone had enough, Jesus gave further instructions: "Gather the pieces that are left over. Let nothing be wasted" (v. 12). And they filled twelve baskets with the pieces of the five barley loaves left over by those who had eaten. They had more at the end than at the beginning. That small lunch became a big lunch in the hands of Jesus.

Years ago I read a Sunday school lesson published by a theologically liberal church. It explained this miracle by saying that when Jesus had the boy's lunch in His hands, others felt ashamed for keeping their food to themselves. Suddenly thousands of little knapsacks appeared, and everyone began to share with everyone else, and a picnic was held on the side of the hill! The point of the story was a lesson on generosity, not Christ's power! How touching!

You feel sorry for those whose god is no greater than a knapsack! The text is clear that the miracle was not that the crowd overcame its selfishness, but that the crowd was fed. Only this explains the twelve baskets left over and why the people wanted to make Jesus a king. Imagine a man at the helm who could create bread!

Jesus departed because He knew that the people wanted to take Him "by force" and make Him a king (v. 15). If they could persuade Him, they would not have to worry about the collapse of the fishing industry or be anxious about the harvest. Jesus would be the answer to their need for physical and economic success. If He wouldn't become a king willingly, they would conscript Him.

Jesus would hear none of it. He was not running for political office. He had a higher agenda; He was en route to the cross and could not be deterred by prospects of a premature coronation. So He withdraws to a mountain to spend time with His heavenly Father.

So much for the miracle. A wonderful miracle, but one that also has a meaning far beyond the benefits thousands of people enjoyed on the hillside. Jesus will now speak to all of us. He will tell us that we also need miracle bread that comes down from heaven.

Let's focus our lens on the spirited discussion that followed this event. Jesus is talking to those who are standing around Him. The dialogue applies to us, for we, also, are the beneficiaries of Jesus' power and supply.

THE DEEPER MESSAGE

The next day, the crowd that had been fed came looking for Jesus. They were hungry again and hoped for another miracle. He read their intentions correctly: "I tell you the truth, you are looking for me, not because you saw miraculous signs but because you ate the loaves and had your fill. Do not work for food that spoils, but for food that endures to eternal life, which the Son of Man will give you. On him God the Father has placed his seal of approval" (vv. 26–27).

No matter how many miracles He did, they hungered for more. "What miraculous sign then will you give that we may see it and believe you? What will you do? Our forefathers ate the manna in the desert; as it is written: 'He gave them bread from heaven to eat'" (vv. 30–31). Prove that you are greater than Moses who gave our ancestors manna! Prove that you can feed us again—and *again!*

Jesus replied, "I tell you the truth, it is not Moses who has given you the bread from heaven, but it is my

Father who gives you the true bread from heaven. For the bread of God is he who comes down from heaven and gives life to the world" (vv. 32–33).

They replied, with a mixture of sincerity and apprehension, "Sir, . . . from now on give us this bread" (v. 34). Yes, in the days of Moses, manna was found on the ground every morning. But the people of Israel had to return for more the next day and the next; it could only satisfy their hunger for the moment. But Jesus is the true bread from heaven who brings fulfillment to the soul. "I am the bread of life. He who comes to me will never go hungry, and he who believes in me will never be thirsty" (v. 35).

Some life-changing lessons emerge from the discussion.

First, *heavenly food is more important than earthly food.* You eat, and you still will die physically; but your soul will live forever. Jesus is not saying, "Stop working and stop eating." He is saying that, in comparison, we should pursue our spiritual diet with more vigor than our physical one.

Elsewhere, Jesus told a story about two men. One was a rich man "dressed in purple and fine linen" who "lived in luxury every day. At his gate was laid a beggar named Lazarus, covered with sores and longing to eat what fell from the rich man's table. Even the dogs came and licked his sores" (Luke 16:19–21).

Incredibly, their fortunes were switched after death. When the beggar died, angels carried him to "Abraham's side" (Luke 16:22). The rich man also died and was buried. "In hell, where he was in torment, he looked up and saw Abraham far away with Lazarus by his side" (v. 23). A conversation ensues, but the future destiny of each man is eternally fixed. The rich man received good things when he was alive; now he was in torment. Lazarus was hungry while on earth but was eminently satisfied in the presence of Abraham and the angels of God.

This story is proof that those who live only for the "food that perishes" will perish with it. Those who seek the heavenly bread will live forever. The difference between the two is time and eternity; heaven and hell.

Second, *the heavenly food can only be found in Jesus.* No other teacher is the "bread from heaven" (John 6:32). Alternatives abound. Our nation is saturated with synthetic junk foods, spiritually speaking. Recently a catalogue arrived at our home featuring such books as *Excavating Your Authentic Self* and *One Day My Soul Just Opened Up* and *Awakening the Buddha Within.* These books share common themes: The soul can heal itself. So if you are hungry, give yourself food; if you are thirsty, dip deeply within yourself and you will be refreshed. We are told to get in touch with "our inner child" so that he or she can be nourished.

But we cannot wipe our own slate clean, be our own Savior, and find within us our spiritual food. Jesus alone can say, "I am the bread of life. He who comes to me will never go hungry, and he who believes in me will never be thirsty" (John 6:35). Heaven is described as the place where "never again will they hunger; never again will they thirst. The sun will not beat upon them, nor any scorching heat. For the Lamb at the center of the throne will be their shepherd; he will lead them to springs of living water" (Revelation 7:16–17). Only Jesus can take us there.

To the New Agers of today who think they have a direct knowledge of God independent of Jesus, He said, "No one has seen the Father except the one who is from God; only he has seen the Father" (John 6:46). You cannot see God without a mediator, priest, and proper sacrifice. The Father knows that only the work of the Son will be successful, and, therefore, only those who trust Him will be eternally satisfied.

Third, *heavenly food is reserved for those who are called to the banquet.* No one can respond to this invitation unless they are drawn to Jesus by the work of the Father. "No one can come to me unless the Father who sent me draws him, and I will raise him up at the last day" (John 6:44). The invitation is open to all, but within that broader circle there is a group of individuals who will come to Christ because they are a gift from the Father to the Son. In this passage of John they are referred to as "all that the Father gives me" (v. 37). Our purpose is not to attempt an explanation of divine sovereignty, but to rejoice in the assurance that God's plan will be accomplished.

The darkness cannot resist the light.

The clay cannot resist the potter.

The creation cannot resist the Creator.

Please don't think that the Father coerces anyone to believe on Jesus. God does not bypass the human will, but works through the will and gives His people the disposition, the desire to believe. That is why Christ could say with confidence, "All that the Father gives me will come to me, and whoever comes to me I will never drive away" (v. 37). Those who come because they are a gift from the Father to the Son will not be driven away. He continues, "For I have come down from heaven not to do my will but to do the will of him who sent me. And this is the will of him who sent me, that I shall lose none of all that he has given me, but raise it up at the last day" (vv. 38–39).

The invitation is given to everyone. Those who are prompted by the Spirit, that is, those who have a desire to come to Jesus, are invited to do so. For those who come, there is fullness, satisfaction, and hope.

No wonder Jesus taught us to pray, "Give us this day our daily bread" (Matthew 6:11; see also Luke 11:3, both KJV). He has proved that He is Lord of our daily needs, Lord of creation, and Lord of all who hunger and thirst. We've just captured a portrait of another miracle that should convince us.

For Further Consideration

Eating Jesus' Flesh and Drinking His Blood

As the discussion between Jesus and the Jews continued, the listeners were divided, some saying that Jesus must be the Messiah, others arguing that what He said was just too difficult to receive. Then, to make matters more contentious, Jesus gave His most controversial speech.

> "I tell you the truth, unless you eat the flesh of the Son of Man and drink his blood, you have no life in you. Whoever eats my flesh and drinks my blood has eternal life, and I will raise him up at the last day. For my flesh is real food and my blood is real drink. Whoever eats my flesh and drinks my blood remains in me, and I in him.

Just as the living Father sent me and I live because of the Father, so the one who feeds on me will live because of me. This is the bread that came down from heaven. Your forefathers ate manna and died, but he who feeds on this bread will live forever." (John 6:53–58)

The meaning of these words has been the focus of controversy throughout the centuries. What does it mean to eat the flesh of the Son of Man and drink His blood?

Many scholars believe that Jesus here anticipated the Lord's Supper, which would be instituted later, the night before He died on the cross.

In the early centuries, the sacraments were called a mystery because they were thought to mediate divine benefits to the worshiper. Just as miracles are "signs" of the visible manifestation of the kingdom, so the sacraments are a "sign," if you will, of the relationship between Jesus and His people. This was particularly true of the Lord's Supper, which began as a simple memorial and then grew to become a complex ritual that was believed to mediate the benefits of Christ to the worshipers.

Given this interpretation of the sacraments, the question naturally arose whether the value of these "signs" was dependent on the priest who blessed the bread and wine or whether they had value "in and of themselves." The church faced a dilemma. If she said that the sacraments were of no merit unless the priest who administered them was living a holy life, the parishioners could never be sure that they were benefiting from these rituals. After all, many priests were known to be outwardly religious but inwardly scandalous. So the church decided that the sacraments contained "within themselves" the value of the grace that they were said to contain. Indeed, they were even of benefit to worshipers regardless of their disposition, as long as they had not committed a mortal sin.

In A.D. 818, Paschasius Radbertus, an abbot of the famous monastery north of Paris at Corbie, published a paper in which he affirmed that the elements were transformed into the literal body and blood of Christ. Though the appearance of the elements does not change, a miracle does take place at the words of the priest: The wine and the bread are transformed into the actual body and blood of the historical Christ. Radbertus affirmed that the outward appearances are but a veil that deceives the senses.

This teaching did not go unchallenged. Theologians such as Rabanus Maurus pointed out that such a belief confuses the sign with that which is signified. The controversy continued more than a hundred years. In the eleventh century, a bishop named Humbert said rather crassly, "The very body of Christ was truly held in the priest's hand and broken and chewed by the teeth of the faithful." Thus the elements were regarded as the very body and blood of Christ. Hildebert of Tours defended this view and called the change of the elements *transubstantiation.*

On the face of it, Jesus cannot have been speaking literally. As D. A. Carson says, "No one would suppose Jesus was seriously advocating cannibalism and offering himself as the first meal."[1] The Law of Moses forbade the drinking of blood and even the eating of meat with the blood still in it. The idea, then, of literally drinking the blood of the Son of Man and eating His flesh was abhorrent. The Jews who took Him literally would, of course, ask, "How can this man give us his flesh to eat?" (John 6:52). Christ answered matter-of-factly, "Unless you eat the flesh of the Son of Man . . . you have no life in you" (v. 53).

Why can we be sure that Christ was not talking literally?

There are several reasons.

First, notice that the one who eats His flesh and drinks His blood "has eternal life, and I will raise him up at the last day" (v. 54). If the result of eating and drinking is to have eternal life, then we should notice that the same result takes place for those who believe in Him. We should not overlook such an obvious connection. "Everyone who looks to the Son and believes in him shall have eternal life, and I will raise him up at the last day" (v. 40). As Carson says, the conclusion is obvious. Eating and drinking the flesh and blood of the Son of Man is a metaphorical way of speaking of those who look to the Son and believe in Him.

In fact, Christ directly associates eating and drinking with believing in Him. "Just as the living Father sent me and I live because of the Father, so the one who feeds on me will live because of me. This is the bread that came down from heaven" (vv. 57–58a). The great theologian Augustine was right when he wrote, "Believe, and you have eaten."

Second, the passage goes on to insist that "the flesh counts for nothing" (v. 63). In context, Jesus is referring back to the controversy His words caused. He reminds them that if we focus on the flesh, the real significance of what is said is misunderstood. Flesh cannot give life: "The Spirit gives life; the flesh counts for nothing. The words I have spoken to you are spirit and they are life" (v. 63). If we rightly respond to what Jesus says, we will believe; and if we believe, we will have life.

Third, if we read this passage carefully, we must conclude that the initiative in salvation rests with Christ. This passage gives no support to those who believe that a priest has the power to transform the elements into the literal body and blood of Christ, and thus has the power to either dispense salvation or withhold it. Throughout the Scriptures the gift of salvation is wrought directly within the human heart in response to faith, apart from rituals.

Finally, if Jesus meant we were to literally eat His flesh and drink His blood, those to whom He spoke had no opportunity to do so, in which case they would not have had "eternal life." Only later would He institute what we call the Lord's Supper; and only after that would there be an opportunity for believers to participate in such a remembrance feast.

The discussion ends with everyone walking away from Christ except for the disciples. "'You do not want to leave too, do you?' Jesus asked the Twelve. Simon Peter answered him: 'Lord, to whom shall we go? You have the words of eternal life. We believe and know that you are the Holy One of God'" (vv. 67–69). This rather disappointing response to His sermon did not catch Christ by surprise. It only reinforced His repeated affirmation that no one can come to Him except that the Father draws him.

Thus the miracle of the loaves and fish leads us to a

deeper spiritual meaning. He who created physical bread is Himself the "bread of life" who gives Himself to a spiritually starved world. To come to Him is to cease to be hungry; to believe on Him is to quench our thirst.

We have good reasons to affirm with Peter, "We believe and know that you are the Holy One of God." (v. 69).

NOTE

1. D. A. Carson, *The Gospel According to John* (Grand Rapids: Eerdmans, 1991), 295.

$\mathcal{J}$esus, Lord of Nature

$\mathcal{W}$e've all seen pictures of the devastating hurricane in Honduras that killed perhaps twelve thousand people and left a half million homeless. Who can begin to calculate the buckets of tears wept in a single hour in the wake of such devastation?

What was God's relationship to this natural disaster? What about earthquakes, tornadoes, and lightning? Is God connected to such events, or should we simply say that they happen with God watching at a distance, letting fallen nature take its course? In the "For Further Consideration" section at the end of this chapter, I shall discuss more specifically God's relationship to such disasters and what we can learn from them. For now, we turn to another miracle, this one proving that Jesus is Lord of nature, both in its fury and in its calm.

In the previous chapter we learned that the disciples found themselves unable to feed the multitude, but, thanks be, Jesus was there to do a miracle. They were eyewitnesses to the power of their Master.

But they still had much to learn about the need for faith, and when they found themselves in a storm on the Sea of Galilee, they needed Jesus more than ever. Whether it was a hungry multitude or a powerful wind, Jesus proved that He was sovereign over both. The lessons the disciples had learned on a calm hillside had to be applied on the stormy sea.

After the feeding of the five thousand, there was a clamor to crown Jesus king. John writes, "Jesus, knowing that they intended to come and make him a king by force, withdrew again to a mountain by himself" (John 6:15). What a king He would be! He could feed the country without effort, rancor, or fanfare! Good-bye fishing and baking bread. Welcome leisure and prosperity!

Once again, Jesus disappointed them by escaping from their presence. He was not seduced by their praise. He calmly compelled His disciples to get into a boat and go ahead of Him to the other side of the lake while He sent the multitudes away. He aborted the plans of the kingmakers and escaped to the hills of Galilee to pray. For seven or eight hours He was in the presence of His Heavenly Father.

As the pole of a compass points north when unobstructed, so the heart of our Lord was constantly seeking the delight of the Father in worship. He seized every opportunity to commune with the One who sent Him. He felt the strain of the crowds, the growing opposition to His messages, and the coming final rejection. There, on the hilltop, the will of the Father was again clarified and the submission of the Son affirmed. He knew that His present job description was to become a savior, not a king.

His decision to send the disciples away alone, was, of course, deliberate. They needed a lesson in faith; they had to know that He was with them, though physically absent. As a mother bird nudges her young ones out of the nest so that they might find their own wings, so Jesus wanted the disciples to be on their own in the coming storm. Though they were beyond the range of His physical sight, those men were still the focus of His care and attention.

They set off toward the west, toward Capernaum; He retired to the hills to pray. If the lesson was faith, and the classroom the turbulent sky, the motivation for the disciples to trust was fear. Usually, the disciples could row across the sea in an hour or two, but this night they were battling the worst storm they could remember. Powerful winds from Mount Hermon lashed the water into a fury, and they were terrified. After seven or eight hours they had gone only three or four miles.

What a journey! The wind buffeted the little boat, and the waves began pounding against the side. Although the disciples were fishermen, they probably had never encountered a storm quite like this. They expected to drown in the very lake they had crossed dozens of times before.

Drenched to the skin, with water blinding their faces, they were so weary they were unable to row any further. They were at the mercy of the elements, waiting for the final lurch that would dash their boat to pieces.

We have rational fears and irrational ones. Irrational fears make no sense to the onlooker; nor do they make sense to the person who is afraid. I've met people who are afraid of crowds, afraid of marriage, or afraid of taking basic necessary risks. Some people, fearing a panic attack, stay indoors.

God created us with the ability to be afraid. Just as surely as He gave us the capacity to love, He gave us the capacity to fear. Properly controlled, fear can protect us from harm. It can keep us from carelessly crossing a street or touching an electrical wire. But if we live with a fear of people, circumstances, or failure, we can be paralyzed, unable to function in this world. John wrote, "Perfect love drives out fear" (1 John 4:18). The disciples had reasons to fear the forces of nature, but if they had listened to Jesus' words more carefully, they could have enjoyed the storm.

When the disciples pushed their boat off and started to row, it was dark, both literally and symbolically. As D. A. Carson says, the darkness of the night and the absence of Jesus are powerfully linked in John's gospel. "By now it was dark, and Jesus had not yet joined them. A strong wind was blowing and the waters grew rough. When they had rowed three or three and a half miles, they saw Jesus approaching the boat, walking on the water; and they were terrified. But he said to them, 'It is I; don't be afraid'" (John 6:17*b*–20).

John gives us a summary of what happened; Matthew adds more details to the same story. "When the disciples saw him walking on the lake, they were terrified. 'It's a ghost,' they said, and cried out in fear" (Matthew 14:26). Even today some people believe that the spirits of the dead return to traverse the earth, haunting different places and frightening people. Yes, there are haunted houses, and "ghosts" that appear pretending to be the spirits of the deceased. More likely, they are demons that masquerade as humans.

The disciples could not relate their experience to anything they had ever encountered. They had never seen anyone walk on water, much less seen a man who had walked on the water for more than three miles. Yet the "ghost" that terrified them was the Jesus who could rescue them.

"Take courage! It is I. Don't be afraid," Jesus told them (Matthew 14:27). John tells us that they were willing to take Him into the boat, "and immediately the boat reached the shore where they were heading" (John 6:21). This phrase seems to imply that there was another miracle, the boat being "immediately" at the shore. With the coming of Jesus, they were back to the safety of land.

They discovered Jesus in the midst of their fears. Even today there are fears within some hearts as terrifying as those that night on the Sea of Galilee. Fear of cancer, fear of poverty, fear of rejection, fear of failure. These fears can torture us, cripple our emotions, and paralyze our ability to function. And yet, in our fright, Jesus comes to us. When we have no strength to row our battered boat, we find Jesus beside us.

LIFE-CHANGING LESSONS
FROM THE SEA OF GALILEE

If we learn the lessons that grow out of this miracle, I promise we will never look at the storms of life in quite the same way again. Here is hope for those who are drowning in circumstances, thinking that the Lord has overlooked them.

He Sees Us

Let's remember that Jesus can see us, even when we cannot see Him! There on the hilltop, He knew the longitude and latitude of their boat; His eye was constantly upon those whom He loved. Perhaps you have learned, as all of us have, that although storms may hide the face of God, yet He is watching us, monitoring our movements.

And when push comes to shove, as it so often does in life, it is more important that God see us than that we see Him. Rest assured His eye is on you as you battle your own personal storm. Though the clouds obscure the face of God, He sees you with impeccable clarity.

Omniscience means all details are known in advance. Unlike our weathermen, Jesus knew the velocity of the wind, its precise direction, and the timing of every gust. He knew the strength of each individual board of the boat and how much battering it could take before it broke apart. *Omnipotence* means that they were battling the storm within the providential will of God. Jesus, as we shall see, was Lord of that storm.

Have you ever noticed how often God brings us to the edge but does not allow us to be taken under? He did not show Abraham the ram when he left home to take that three-day journey. God did not show him the ram after he built the altar, nor when he laid his son on the altar. The ram was seen only after Abraham raised his knife to kill his favorite son, Isaac. God often has a ram in the bush, but we see it only in the nick of time. At just the right moment, Jesus arrives.

What if the boat had broken apart and the disciples

had drowned that night? We know this could not have happened because Jesus still had work for them to do. But we can be assured of this: If they had drowned, their death would have been just as much God's will as their rescue was.

Death does not sever us from the love of Jesus, nor does it sever us from His protection. Remember, He is there even when we do not see Him.

He Leads Us

Obedience, yes, I said *obedience,* often puts us in the path of a storm. Jesus sent them into danger so that they might be delivered from a greater danger, namely, the temptation to be swept away with the crowd. Let us never forget that it was Jesus who asked them to go to the other side. It was the Master of the winds who planned that they would row directly into a storm.

If the disciples had clung to Jesus' every word, they could have enjoyed their battle against the waves, absolutely assured that no harm would come to them. Why? Because when Jesus said good-bye to them that evening, He expressly told them to "go on ahead of him to the other side" (Matthew 14:22). If the Master of the universe said that they were to arrive on Galilee's shore, they should have known that come what may, they would make it! Some of those disciples had been chosen to die a martyr's death, so there was no chance that they would drown that evening. No wonder Jesus said to Peter, "You of little faith, . . . why did you doubt?" (Matthew 14:31). If only they had listened and believed, their fear would have vanished.

Sometimes we have the mistaken notion that a

storm is proof that we are "out of the will of God." Yet, it is in the center of God's will, in obedience to Him, that we might encounter the fiercest opposition. Let's not fall into the error of thinking that we have made a wrong decision just because we are sailing into high winds. Sometimes our greatest trial comes when we are walking in obedience to the Lord's command.

You say, "But I'm in a storm today of my own making." Your storm might not be those external circumstances you cannot control but the circumstances of a bad decision, the circumstances that resulted from your own foolishness and sins.

What then?

The answer, thankfully, is that Jesus is as willing to help you in the storm that is your fault as He is to help you in a storm created by circumstances, or a storm created because of what someone else has done. Jonah learned that even if we are in a storm of our own making, God has not forsaken us. He is there, tracking our every move. Our Savior will pray for us and come to us in our time of need.

I speak to the young unmarried woman who is pregnant; I speak to the gambler who lost his money; I speak to the marriage partner who has been unfaithful; I speak to those who have experienced failure because of personal fears. Where is God when you are living with the dark consequences of your own making? Yes, God stands ready to help in circumstances that you have brought upon yourself.

Just ask Adam. With the devastation caused by his sin lying all around him, he did not know where to turn. But God graciously "made garments of skin" to cover his nakedness (Genesis 3:21) and instituted sacrifices so that his sin could be forgiven. Though it was his fault that paradise turned into a swamp, God was there for him.

And God is there for you and me.

He Is with Us

Today Jesus is not praying on a mountaintop, but He is sitting at the right hand of God the Father in heaven. As our High Priest, He remembers us to the Father. And by His Spirit, He walks with us through the storms. Fear has a way of distorting our perception. In our fear we cannot tell friend from foe. We see ghosts, but we don't see Jesus. We see darkness, but we don't see light.

The disciples would tell us that the very object we fear might be Jesus coming toward us. This terrifying ghost, this phantom, was a hidden blessing. Dr. Harry Ironside of Moody Church used to tell the story that illustrates the point. He would get on his hands and knees and chase his three-year-old son around the room, all the while growling like a bear. Then one day when the little boy was backed into a corner, he rushed into his father's arms and said, "You're not a bear, you're my papa!"

The fear that seems to march toward us just might be God attempting to put His arms around us. The object we fear loses its power if we see God in the midst of it. How blessed to hear the words of Jesus, "It is I; don't be afraid" (John 6:20).

Is it possible to see God in cancer? Ask those who have been drawn close to Him when they were told that their life was on the line. Can we see God in the breakup of a marriage or the untimely death of a child?

Yes, even here we believe that He is with us. Blessed are those who know that Jesus does not abandon His people in the midst of the storm.

On the hillside, the Good Shepherd had the people enjoy the green pastures; now He led them by the still waters. The Lord of our daily bread is the Lord of our circumstances.

He Triumphs over Our Adversity

The disciples expected to drown; they could visualize the water surging above their heads as they sank to the bottom of the Sea of Galilee. But the water that threatened to be over their head was under Jesus' feet. The waves that would drown them became like a marble slab under the feet of the Son of God.

Think about your storm. Whether it is your health, your finances, your vocation, or your relationships—that situation, no matter how painful, is one that Jesus has fully under His control. Let us see Jesus crushing the devil and inviting us to join Him in the victory! Let us see Jesus walking over the sea of God's wrath and inviting us to join Him. Let us see Jesus triumphing over the sting of death and inviting us to join Him!

Even if the wind is calm, we will still drown if we fail to look at Jesus. Hugh Martin wrote, "You will sink through the waters when the wind be boisterous or blow softly from the south. In either case it matters not. But if you stand firm on the waters in Christ's name, sharing His dominion over sin, the curse, Satan, the world, and death—oh! Then no danger can arise from the wind: it must all be from unbelief."[1]

Matthew tells us that Peter asked Jesus' permission

to walk toward his Master, meeting Him on the water. "But when he saw the wind, he was afraid and, beginning to sink, cried out 'Lord, save me!'" (Matthew 14:30). Why did he shift his eyes away from Jesus? He had a moment of self-awareness, the sensation that he was doing what under normal conditions is impossible. He knew that the wind and the waves were more powerful than he; he was not Lord of nature. Yet, there he was, for a brief moment walking on water with his Master. But then *he failed because he looked away from Jesus.*

A high wire performer said that he must walk the wire concentrating completely on a fixed point on the other side. If his attention is diverted, he could lose his balance. Concentration is the key to walking where others have fallen. And how long did it take for Peter to sink when he looked at the wind? Perhaps a second or two. I have had to learn that a few moments of broken fellowship with Jesus can cause me to drown in a storm that could destroy me. The strength of Satan or the intensity of our trials is not what forces us to fall; *unbelief is always our mortal enemy.*

Tony Evans tells the story of when he and his wife were on a cruise to Alaska and encountered high winds en route. The captain told the passengers that they were headed into high winds, so everyone was to prepare for the choppy seas. Later, as the boat rocked, Tony's wife, Lois, was angry and sent a message to the captain, "Why did you take the ship into the storm? Could we not have waited?" The message was received by an assistant, who promised to relay her concerns to the captain and get back to her. Moments later, the phone in the room rang and the assistant said, "I relayed your concerns to the captain, and he told me to tell you to relax because this ship was built with this storm in mind."

When we believe in Jesus we are on a boat headed to the other side. Along the way, the waves batter us; the boards are creaking, and the ship is jostling. *But this ship was built with our storms in mind.*

Those who trust in Jesus discover Him to be as good as His word.

For Further Consideration

The Role of God in Nature

On the Sea of Galilee, Jesus proved that He is the King of nature, the One who speaks to the wind and suddenly there is a "great calm." And when He speaks to the water, it becomes pavement under His feet. What, then, is the relationship between Jesus and other manifestations of nature, such as earthquakes, tornadoes, and floods? Is nature out of control, or does it act under the supervision of God and His purposes?

After an earthquake in California some years ago, a group of ministers met for a prayer breakfast. Several of them spoke and agreed on one thing: God had nothing to do with the earthquake that rocked their city. Yet, incredibly, as they closed in prayer they thanked God that the earthquake came early in the morning before the morning rush hour when so many more would have been killed!

So, did God have anything to do with the California earthquake or didn't He? What is His relationship to natural disasters? The biblical answer, of course, is that earthquakes are "permitted," or ordained, by God (after all, He could have chosen to *not* permit it), according to the good pleasure of His will. Even if He should use the devil to do His bidding, the Almighty still controls the details of what the Evil One can or cannot do. In other words, God is the One who rules, and He must give the "go ahead" for every movement of nature.

Let us affirm that the earth is God's creation. He spoke the worlds into existence; He created the sun and the moon and established the seasons. And He who created the earth did not abandon it after the Fall.

When the sons of Korah rebelled against Moses, the Lord had this message for them:

> "If these men die a natural death and experience only what usually happens to men, then the Lord has not sent me. But if the Lord brings about something totally new, and the earth opens its mouth and swallows them, with everything that belongs to them, and they go down alive into the grave, then you will know that these men have treated the Lord with contempt." (Numbers 16:29–30)

Immediately the ground beneath them split apart and the earth swallowed them alive. It was God who did it.

Who sent the Flood during the time of Noah? Who determined its intensity, area, and time of duration?

Who sent darkness that could be felt during the plagues of Egypt and, centuries later, sent added sunshine so Joshua would have time to win the war against the Amalekites?

Who allowed Satan to send the wind to destroy Job's ten children?

Who sent the storm that caused the sailors to throw Jonah overboard?

Who sent hurricane Mitch to Honduras, killing some twelve thousand people and leaving millions homeless? If we say that it was not God (as some will want to affirm), then we not only contradict Scripture but are left with an impossible conclusion: The God who knows the number of hairs on our heads—the God who watches the sparrow fall—allowed an entire country to be devastated without His express consent.

We are hesitant to affirm that it is God who did such things because we are anxious to defend His reputation. We want to absolve Him from any responsibility for such disasters. Interestingly, the Scriptures never feel this pressure to distance God from the happenings of planet Earth. "When disaster comes to a city, has not the Lord caused it?" (Amos 3:6*b*). The prophet wants us to answer, "Yes, the Lord did it."

But why? Why the separation of families, the children weeping for their dead parents, mothers finding the cold body of a son or daughter in the debris of an earthquake or at the bottom of a flooded street?

Surely there are some clues in Scripture regarding the purpose of it all. Jesus Himself helps us put it in perspective.

THE MESSAGE OF NATURAL DISASTERS

When Jesus was told about some Galileans whose blood Pilate had mixed with their sacrifices, He set the record straight: Those who died were not greater sinners than others in Jerusalem. That, of course, is easy to accept. Dying the death of a martyr is an honor and possibly a mark of a deep religious commitment rather than a sign of spiritual rebellion or apostasy.

But then Jesus continued, "Or those eighteen who died when the tower in Siloam fell on them—do you think they were more guilty than all the others living in Jerusalem? I tell you, no! But unless you repent, you too will all perish" (Luke 13:4–5).

We must never think that these disasters prove that the victims are worse sinners than others are, and therefore they "deserved" their fate. Natural disasters do send a message to the world, but we must be careful to understand what that message is.

An increase in earthquakes in California does not mean that Californians are greater sinners than others in America. A hurricane in Honduras does not mean that that country is more wicked than neighboring Guatemala.

I saw pictures of a church that was spared the wrath of a tornado, and the congregation had a prayer service, thanking God that their lives were spared. But I have also seen church buildings devastated by a tornado; God did not protect His people or His building.

In this life the sun shines on the righteous as well as the wicked, and earthquakes come indiscriminately to both groups. We dare not judge the spiritual standings of those whose lives are cut down by the violence of nature. God has other purposes for these supposedly random acts. Indeed, His purpose is so specific that they are random only from our point of view, not His.

What lessons do these disasters teach us? Every natural disaster is E-mail from God to us. His lessons should be clear for all to see.

First, *death is inevitable.* When we see the obituary

of someone who died in a flood, we should see our own name in the column. We are all in the process of dying. Some day we too shall die; we will have our names in the newspaper, if our relatives remember to take note of our passing.

Every funeral is a reminder of our own mortality. But a violent death heightens our awareness; it jerks us back to reality; it is a sermon from God telling us that our death is as sure as the sunrise. A couple who moved from California to the Midwest for fear of earthquakes died in a tornado in Kansas.

C. S. Lewis said that war does not increase death; the people who died would have died anyway, even if at a later date. The same can be said for those who die in natural disasters; they also would have died at a later date. Death is around us, and we cannot escape its reality; we are reminded of how quickly it comes when a friend dies without warning.

Second, *natural disasters are a picture of judgment to come.* "Unless you repent, you will all likewise perish" (Luke 13:5 NASB). That word *likewise* does not mean that the unrepentant will die in a similar disaster. It means that they will die with the same certainty and unexpectedness. They will suddenly be gone as in a moment.

During the tribulation period, God will use natural disasters as a means of judgment.

> I watched as he opened the sixth seal. There was a great earthquake. The sun turned black like sackcloth made of goat hair, the whole moon turned blood red, and the stars in the sky fell to earth, as late figs drop from a fig tree when shaken by a strong wind. The sky

receded like a scroll, rolling up, and every mountain and island was removed from its place.

Then the kings of the earth, the princes, the generals, the rich, the mighty, and every slave and every free man hid in caves and among the rocks of the mountains. They called to the mountains and the rocks, "Fall on us and hide us from the face of him who sits on the throne and from the wrath of the Lamb! For the great day of their wrath has come, and who can stand?" (Revelation 6:12–17)

We all know the story of the Titanic, that huge ship that hit an iceberg and sank beneath the icy waters of the Atlantic. As it was sinking, people cried to God for perhaps two hours, pleading that He spare their lives. If God did not listen to the cries of 1,522 people who pled for His mercy, what does that teach us about the judgment to come?

If God did not intervene in the Holocaust, a terrible disaster carried out by evil men; if the Almighty could watch and not respond to the suffering of the children weeping for their parents, then it is not difficult for me to believe in hell. A God who can witness these disasters and not answer the pleas of desperate people can indeed judge unbelievers and consign them to an eternal fate.

Natural disasters are God's message sent from heaven: Wake up! Something far worse is on its way.

Third, *to escape future judgment we must repent*. "Unless you repent, you too will all perish" (Luke 13:5 NASB). In the United States we have divided our people into Republicans and Democrats, black and white, young and old, rich and poor. But in the Day of Judgment, the human race will be divided into just two categories: the repentant and the unrepentant, the saved and the lost, those in heaven and those in hell.

Repentance means that we change our minds about God and about ourselves. We admit our sinfulness and our inability to save ourselves. We transfer our trust to Jesus, knowing that apart from Him we would be lost forever.

Jesus caused the storm on the Sea of Galilee; Jesus stilled the storm on the Sea of Galilee. When He returns to the Mount of Olives, it shall split in two, causing a deep valley near Jerusalem (Zechariah 14:3–4). Indeed, at His return, "the sign of the Son of Man will appear in the sky, and all the nations of the earth will mourn. They will see the Son of Man coming on the clouds of the sky, with power and great glory" (Matthew 24:30).

Jesus walked on water, not just to rescue the disciples whom He loved, but to remind us that "God [has] placed all things under his feet" (Ephesians 1:22).

Jesus actually is God; He is not just applying for the job.

NOTE

1. Hugh Martin, *Simon Peter* (Carlisle, Pa.: Banner of Truth, 1967), 51–52.

$\mathcal{J}$esus, Lord of Future Judgment

$\mathcal{N}$othing touches our hearts like a child with a congenital defect. An infant born crippled or deformed generates pity in even the hardest heart. A child born blind will never see the light of day; he will never enjoy the beauty of nature or even see his parents and siblings. Imagine the darkness of it all.

To see such a child is to come face-to-face with questions about God. How could He allow such suffering? If the Father loves children, as Jesus claimed, why would He allow such disabilities when a command from His lips would cause the blind to see and the deaf to hear?

Human suffering has pushed some thinkers into the arms of atheism. "If God can see such suffering and not intervene, then He either does not exist or He is the devil," I've heard it said. Scary indeed, for if God does not exist, then we shall never have an answer to the problem of suffering, neither in this life nor the life to come. And if He does exist but is as cruel as the devil, then we are without hope. After all, a sovereign malevolent being cannot be trusted and might decree that all of us suffer forever.

There is a more satisfying answer to the problem of suffering, and that is to say that God is both powerful and good, but uses human suffering to a higher end. He desires to display the wonder of His love and grace in this life and will especially do so in the life to come.

Jesus encountered a man born blind, a man whose story illustrates how God uses suffering for a higher end. "As he went along, he saw a man blind from birth. His disciples asked him, 'Rabbi, who sinned, this man or his parents, that he was born blind?'" (John 9:1–2).

His reply was startling, "Neither this man nor his parents sinned, . . . but this happened so that the work of God might be displayed in his life. As long as it is day, we must do the work of him who sent me. Night is coming, when no one can work. While I am in the world, I am the light of the world" (vv. 3–5).

Of course Jesus was not saying that this man and his parents never sinned; He was simply saying that this man's blindness was not the result of personal sin. We can say generally that there is a connection between sin and suffering; that is, all suffering is the result of the Fall. But we have no right to make a tight connection between the two; we cannot look at a suffering person and say that his pain is greater because his sin is greater. There *might* be such a connection, but given our limited knowledge we have no right to make such a judgment.

Occasionally the Scriptures make such relationships, but in this instance Jesus explicitly denied that this man's condition was because of personal sin.

The disciples' question does not mean that they believed in reincarnation. They were not saying that the man himself could have sinned in some previous existence which resulted in his blindness. They asked whether his blindness was the result of his sin (some of the rabbis believed it was possible for a fetus to participate in the sin of the pregnant mother who worshiped in a pagan temple), or if his parents sinned in some way as to cause this malady. Their question did, however, imply that they thought there was a tight connection between sin and this man's disability.

As we've learned, Jesus disavowed the direct connection and gave a different rationale: "Neither this man nor his parents sinned, . . . but this happened so that the work of God might be displayed in his life" (vv. 3–4). Difficult though it is to believe, this man's blindness had a divine purpose. This happened so that "the work of God" might be displayed in his life.

THE WORKS OF GOD IN A BLIND MAN

What was the "work of God" (or the plural, "works of God," NASB) to which Jesus referred? If we read the story carefully, we discover at least three "works" Jesus demonstrated through this man's experience.

Physical Healing

Put yourself in this man's sandals. He had never seen his mother or father; he had never seen a sunset; he had never seen his friends. His was a dark world where others could easily take advantage of him. Discrimination, rejection, and humiliation were his constant companions. He would have to sit patiently as others described what it was like to see their surroundings. He never dared dream that he himself would someday see as well as they.

The idea that his life was lived within the bounds of God's providential care never crossed his mind. He would receive a blessing he never thought possible, and his story would occupy a full chapter in God's Holy Word. Not once did he think he was destined for such a high calling.

Jesus "saw a man," John tells us. Of course, He saw many men, men who could see and at least some who were blind. From the crowd He chose *this* one, a man who was destined for *this* day and *this* hour. The story reminds us that God's work among us is individualized; ultimately, it is just you and Jesus; just Jesus and me.

Jesus used a procedure recorded nowhere else in His earthly ministry. "Having said this, he spit on the ground, made some mud with the saliva, and put it on the man's eyes. 'Go,' he told him, 'wash in the Pool of Siloam' (this word means Sent). So the man went and washed, and came home seeing" (vv. 6–7).

Why this rather crude method? Probably because there were certain taboos connected with saliva, and Jesus often broke with customs to show that they in themselves were not universal. Of course, He could have healed the man without using the mud. Though mud might have healing properties, it does not have the power to take a blind man and cause him to see! The power was not in the mud, but in the person of Jesus.

Nor would Jesus have had to send him to the pool of Siloam to wash. Again, the healing power was not in the water, but in Jesus' word. But instructions are instructions, so the man took Jesus at His word. He either asked a friend to help him find the pool, or he hesitatingly inched his way along the path, choosing a familiar route. With anticipation, he stooped down and washed the mud from his eyes. He noticed the ripples in the shallow water.

He could see!

The man's neighbors were dumbfounded! They asked one another, "Isn't this the same man who used to sit and beg?" (v. 8). Some said, "Yes"; others said, "No."

But, of course, the man himself insisted, "I am the man" (v. 9).

So they pressed him to tell how his eyes were opened.

"The man they call Jesus made some mud and put it on my eyes. He told me to go to Siloam and wash. So I went and washed, and then I could see" (v. 11).

Of course they didn't believe a word of it!

The man with congenital blindness made his living begging, so they knew him well. They saw him every day, standing in the corners, hand outstretched, hoping for a denarius. Now they found it easier to believe that he had disappeared and that the man before them was somebody else. "He only *looks* like him," they insisted.

What follows is one of the most interesting and even humorous passages in all the Bible. The interchange between the man and the Jews, the man and his parents, and again the parents and the Jews makes for a fascinating glimpse into human nature.

Word spread, and the neighbors begin by interrogating the newly healed man; then they brought him to the Jews to find out what had *really* happened (vv. 13–17).

The man answered, "He put mud on my eyes, . . . and I washed, and now I see" (v. 15).

The Pharisees were unimpressed, "This man is not from God, for he does not keep the Sabbath" (v. 16). Apparently they assumed that Jesus, in making this bit of mud, was breaking the Sabbath. At any rate, in their minds, all healings were forbidden on the Sabbath, no matter how they were performed. So they concluded that even if the man was healed, the miracle could not possibly be from God.

But not everyone was buying what the Pharisees were selling. The growing crowd asked, "'How can a sinner do such miraculous signs?' So they were divided" (v. 16).

The frustrated Jews talked to the blind man again. "What have you to say about him? It was your eyes he opened" (v. 17).

"He is a prophet," the man replied, grasping for the right word to describe the Healer he met along the path. It was his best guess.

The Jews still did not believe that this actually was the same man who had been born blind, so they called his parents. "Is this your son? . . . Is this the one you say was born blind? How is it that now he can see?" (v. 19).

"'We know he is our son,' the parents answered, 'and we know he was born blind. But how he can see now, or who opened his eyes, we don't know. Ask him. He is of age; he will speak for himself'" (vv. 20–21).

John adds that his parents said this because they

were afraid of the Jews, who had said that if anyone accepted Jesus as the Christ he would be put out of the synagogue. They did not want to get involved in the theological traps the Pharisees had set up. So they confessed ignorance.

Again, the Pharisees summoned the man who had been blind and with impeccable human rationality began by separating the miracle from the Miracle Worker. "'Give glory to God. . . . We know this man [Jesus] is a sinner" (v. 24).

If this healed man thought others would share his joy, he was mistaken. He was exasperated by their interrogation. He whose life was so profoundly changed by the word of Jesus, now professed no competence to judge whether or not Jesus was a sinner. That was a matter for the theological experts. But he was sure of one point, "Whether he is a sinner or not, I don't know. One thing I do know. I was blind but now I see!" (v. 25). Yes, all that he knew was that there was a huge difference between blindness and sight, darkness and light!

Again, they asked him how the miracle happened. He replied by saying that he had already told them, so why should he repeat his story? Then he agitated them with this verbal missive, "Do you want to become his disciples, too?" (v. 27).

With that he crossed the line.

"Then they hurled insults at him and said, 'You are this fellow's disciple! We are disciples of Moses! We know that God spoke to Moses, but as for this fellow [Jesus], we don't even know where he comes from'" (v. 28).

The healed man was not without words! He continues, with more than just a touch of sarcasm, "Now that is remarkable! You don't know where he comes from, yet he has opened my eyes. We know that God does not listen to sinners. He listens to the godly man who does his will. Nobody has ever heard of opening the eyes of a man born blind. If this man were not from God, he could do nothing" (vv. 30–33).

Ouch.

"'You were steeped in sin at birth; how dare you lecture us!' And they threw him out" (v. 34).

They had a miracle on their hands for which they had no explanation. Rather than conclude that Jesus was from God, they expelled the man who caused them grief. They could not rejoice in a healed blind man if it meant they had to revise their opinion of Jesus.

Why was this man born blind? His healing would force the closed-minded Pharisees to make up their mind about Jesus. "So they were divided" (v. 16), John tells us. The man benefited from the healing, and those who loved Jesus benefited too. They had an opportunity to declare their faith in the heat of theological controversy.

Jesus' enemies had a chance to declare themselves too, but their deeply held prejudices against Him were hardened in the heat of the battle. From now on, they would begin to plan to put Jesus to death.

One work of God had been accomplished. The man born blind was healed. Even if few rejoiced at his new life, he went to bed with a new set of eyes. And when he awoke in the morning, he discovered it was not a dream.

But before nightfall he met the man who had healed him. And what a discovery this happy man made!

Spiritual Conversion

When Jesus heard that they had thrown the man out, He "found" him. Jesus went looking for him, so that the man would have an opportunity to declare his faith. Jesus asked,

> "Do you believe in the Son of Man?"
>
> "Who is he sir?" the man asked. "Tell me so that I may believe in him."
>
> Jesus said, "You have now seen him; in fact, he is the one speaking with you."
>
> Then the man said, "Lord, I believe," and he worshiped him. (vv. 35–38)

Many gracious works of God often precede conversion. In this case it was the miracle of healing. The fact that this man did not know who healed him is further proof that Jesus healed some people quite apart from their faith and quite apart from their knowledge of who He was. He "found" this man and told him to go wash—and he obeyed and was healed. If the first work of God was that of healing, the second was that of conversion. And the latter was a much greater miracle than the former.

The physically blind can often see better than those who have 20/20 vision. I remember a man in my home church who was blind from birth. Whenever the microphone was open for "testimony" time, he would stand to his feet, steady himself with his right hand on the church pew, and talk about God's faithfulness. Then he would add, "Just to think—the first person I will ever see is the Lord Jesus Christ."

That man died many years ago, and his eyesight is better than yours or mine. What a revelation, what joy, what fulfillment! Years ago we used to sing a song titled, "It Will Be Worth It All, When We See Jesus." This man would tell us that, yes, it is worth it all.

Better to live in darkness in this life than to live in darkness in the life to come. We are more blessed through the miracle of conversion than we ever could be through the miracle of restored eyesight. It's the difference of eternity and time; eternal bliss and temporary inconvenience and suffering.

What miracles Jesus accomplished! A blind man was made to see, and a sinful heart became a "new heart" by the power of Jesus. The words the man spoke are precious: "Lord, I believe" (v. 38).

And he worshiped Christ.

The Judgment of the World

If this man had been born blind just so he could meet Jesus and be converted, his suffering would have been worth it.

But there is more to the story.

Jesus used the blind man to illustrate His purpose for coming into the world. To put it simply, He came to give spiritual sight to those who admit that they are spiritually blind, and He came to confirm the blindness of those who self-righteously think they can see. Listen to His own words: "For judgment I have come into this world, so that the blind will see and those who see will become blind" (John 9:39).

In the first instance, the blind are spiritually needy and willingly admit it. Because they see themselves for what they are and, therefore, depend on Jesus, they are given spiritual sight. He is always attracted to weakness, helplessness, and great neediness.

But those who think they see, and therefore reject the light, such will "become blind." So certain are they that they can see, that they find no reason to call upon Jesus for healing their souls. In fact, for now, their blindness is more comfortable than the distressing prospect of exposure to light.

The contrast is between this man who knew he was blind and was therefore healed physically, and the Pharisees who were blind spiritually but refused to admit it. Reread this chapter and you will find them to be self-assured, puffed up with knowledge, joyless, and content with themselves. So their darkness remains.

To put it simply: An acknowledgement of spiritual blindness is indispensable to benefiting from Jesus' healing power. We've all met people who think they are quite fine, thank you. They call their sins "failures," and their glaring hypocrisy, "imperfections." They congratulate themselves for finding the path on their own.

These stand in contrast to the people who are only too aware of their glaring need for God's forgiveness and gracious acceptance. These humble, repentant sinners are given eyes to see.

The Pharisees understood what Jesus was saying but were not prepared to admit their blindness. With a touch of sarcasm they asked, "What? Are we blind too?" (v. 40). Jesus replied, "If you were blind, you would not be guilty of sin; but now that you claim you can see, your guilt remains" (v. 41).

We could paraphrase His words, "If you were blind and cried out for illumination, you would not be guilty of sin (particularly the sin of unbelief). But now that you claim to see, you still remain in your sins; your blindness remains."

Thus the third "work of God" is revealed. It is the work of judgment. This miracle illustrates how the brilliant shining of the true Light can make the blind to be even "more blind." The self-righteous hate the light, withdrawing to their own secret deeds, more determined than ever that they will not be exposed. As in the days of Moses, their darkness is so deep it can almost be "felt."

> "This is the verdict: Light has come into the world, but men loved darkness instead of the light because their deeds were evil. Everyone who does evil hates the light, and will not come into the light for fear that his deeds will be exposed. But whoever lives by the truth comes into the light, so that it may be seen plainly that what he has done has been done through God." (John 3:19–21)

Not all people are made better when they encounter Jesus. He leaves some people worse than He finds them. The blind are confirmed in their blindness; they now incur the judgement of Jesus. Having rejected the light, they might never be exposed to it again.

Was it fair for this man to be born blind just for the purposes of this illustration? Imagine years of darkness and hopelessness just because Jesus wanted to display His power and make a point about spiritual darkness!

It was worth the wait. The years of discrimination

and discouragement were nothing in comparison to the joy and the challenge. Today his suffering has vanished in the light of a radiant eternity.

But what about the blind person who is never healed? What about the person who never sees the light of day and the one who dies in obscurity without being an illustration of anything? If those persons come to faith in Jesus, their blindness will be made up to them. "I consider that our present sufferings are not worth comparing with the glory that will be revealed in us" (Romans 8:18).

If you suffer from a disability, keep in mind that you suffer within the sphere of God's providential will. I know this is difficult to accept; we balk at the mystery of God's purposes; but it is true nevertheless.

Moses, you will recall, was arguing with God, giving reasons why he should not be conscripted to go into Egypt to deliver the Israelites. He told the Lord that he was not eloquent, but rather was "slow of speech and tongue" (Exodus 4:10).

The Lord responded, "Who gave man his mouth? Who makes him deaf or mute? Who gives him sight or makes him blind? Is it not I, the Lord?" (v. 11).

Fanny Crosby was not born blind. At the age of a few months, a doctor suggested to her parents that a certain kind of salve be used for a rash around her eyes. This procedure blinded her. She did not experience the healing of the blind man in Jerusalem. Yet at the age of nine she wrote:

> O, what a happy soul I am,
> Although I cannot see:
> I am resolved that in this world

Contented I will be.
How many blessings I enjoy
That other people don't;
To weep and sigh, because I'm blind—
I cannot and I won't.

She saw better than most because she trusted the Light of this World. Jesus gave her spiritual light, and that is what really mattered. "For our light and momentary troubles are achieving for us an eternal glory that far outweighs them all. So we fix our eyes not on what is seen, but on what is unseen. For what is seen is temporary, but what is unseen is eternal" (2 Corinthians 4:17–18).

Only Jesus can make the blind to see, the deaf to hear, and the crippled to walk.

For Further Consideration

Divine Healing and the Atonement

The fact that Jesus healed so many people has led some to conclude that divine healing is the prerogative of every Christian. Some faith healers teach that it is God's will for every Christian to be healed, at all times. This teaching needs evaluation.

Many years ago I attended a healing service conducted by Kathryn Kuhlman, the famous faith healer of a past era. Throughout her message she kept saying that people should be expecting healing even as she spoke; only the healed were to come forward to "claim their healing." Near the end of her message, several came forward to say, "I have been healed."

One man, in particular, caught my attention. He had come to the meeting in a wheelchair, but now was walking with stooped shoulders across the stage, acknowledging the cheers of the crowd. When he came down from the platform, I motioned to him and asked what he had been healed of. He whispered in my ear, "I'm not sure I'm healed yet, but I am trusting the Lord for healing."

"So you were able to walk before you came here today," I asked. "Yes, but I walk with difficulty." That night thousands of people went home from the meeting and told their friends, "I saw a man healed with my own eyes!"

Another man who claimed his "healing" said he was of the Muslim faith; others said they were healed of back pains, smoking, and alcoholism. Most heartbreaking, however, was to see hundreds of people in wheelchairs wheeled back to the buses that had come from Milwaukee, Detroit, and Saint Louis. Perhaps it had just been a difficult day for the faith healer, but I was not convinced that anyone had been healed that long afternoon, though of course, only God knows for sure.

Faith healers have a ready answer for those who are not healed: It is the *seeker's* lack of faith. No fault on the part of the faith healer, of course. It is the absence of faith in those who come for healing! Yes, Mark said that Jesus would not do many miracles because of "unbelief," but on a personal level, Jesus never tried to heal a person only to turn away because he or she did not have enough faith. Indeed, as we have learned, He often healed people sovereignly without demanding any faith at all.

That afternoon I also witnessed firsthand what is now common among the faith healers seen on television. Those who came to the platform were touched by the evangelist and "slain in the spirit." They fell backward, caught by ushers and laid on the floor. After a few moments they "came to" and left the platform area walking on their own strength. This phenomenon, though widely practiced today, is neither found in the New Testament nor practiced by the apostles. To appeal to the story of the soldiers who "fell backward" when they came to capture Christ to justify this modern novelty is to misuse the Scriptures. Of course, Christ the Son of God can smite soldiers if He so desires, but these Romans who fell backward were certainly not "filled" or "slain with the Spirit." Much less can this account be used to justify some kind of supernatural power that strikes when the faith healer touches his followers.

All of this raises some relevant questions: Does the Bible teach that we can be healed anytime we have the faith to "claim our healing"? Are there promises that we can take for our personal healing and the healing of others?

THE PROMISES OF GOD

We must humbly admit that there are no promises that say we can be healed whenever we wish if only we had the faith. If there were, we would not have to die until the Lord returns. We could just keep claiming our healing again and again. You should not be surprised that there are people today who think that an endless life is indeed possible, based on divine promises. I knew a man, who has since died, who believed that he would live until the Lord returned. But even the faith healer he most admired is now dead.

"Every promise in the book is mine," we used to sing as children. But it is simply not true. Abraham received promises that were not meant for us; the disciples were given promises that they would sit on twelve thrones judging the twelve tribes of Israel. I have no intention of "claiming these promises." We must determine which promises are ours, and then find out what they actually say.

The best-known promises for divine healing are found in Isaiah 53, which is quoted in Matthew 8:17. There we read that Christ went about healing people "to fulfill what was spoken through the prophet Isaiah: 'He took up our infirmities and carried our diseases.'" Peter wrote, "He himself bore our sins in his body on the tree, so that we might die to sins and live for righteousness; by his wounds you have been healed" (1 Peter 2:24).

Some theologians who are skeptical of divine healing have labored to prove that the healing spoken of in these passages is spiritual, not physical. But the context in Matthew and the implication of Peter is that Christ did indeed die for our physical bodies. In fact, it is consistent with Scripture to affirm that Christ came to redeem the whole man—body, soul, and spirit.

But does this mean that we can have physical healing whenever we prayerfully meet the conditions? Clearly the answer is no. Although Christ died for our bodies as well as our souls, we will not see the fulfillment of that aspect of our redemption until we are resurrected into glory. Christ came to redeem us from sin, but we still have a sin nature; He came to destroy death, yet we die; He came to redeem our bodies, yet we are subject to accidents, poisons, and the frailty of the flesh. Our resurrected body is in the atonement, but today the body we carefully nurture is subject to disease. Yes, of course, some day the enemy of death will be taken away, but we aren't there yet.

Many who teach that divine healing is instantly available wear glasses, get arthritis, and have implanted hearing aids. All these infirmities bear eloquent testimony to the fact that in this life we see only the beginning of redemption. Yes, sometimes God does heal (particularly as seen in the ministry of Christ), but even then, the healing is merely a postponement of future illness and death. Even Christ's healings on earth were not permanent. The people He healed, died.

This misunderstanding of the promises of Scripture has been the source of much grief in the Christian community. People who claim healing, insisting that God is obligated to keep His promises, often end up feeling betrayed. When healing does not occur, they point to these verses and say that God cannot be trusted. Or they try to find some other reason, such as unbelief, unconfessed sin, and so on, to explain why they were not healed. Since they believe they have heard God correctly, they take the fault upon themselves to protect His reputation.

Others point to the promise of James that the sick should call for the elders of the church to pray. If the sick one is anointed with oil, "the prayer offered in faith will make the sick person well; the Lord will raise him up. If he has sinned, he will be forgiven" (5:15). This cannot mean that a believer will always be raised up; if it did, we would be back to saying that a person could escape death indefinitely. He could just keep calling for the elders of the church.

The answer to this prayer is actually dependent on the "prayer of faith," which means that in specific instances God may grant the elders the united faith to believe in the restoration of the individual. In other instances they might not have such faith. The "raising up" takes place only when God grants the gift of faith for that particular situation. It is impossible for us to manufacture such faith on our own.

Other promises related to prayer come to mind. Christ said to His disciples, "And I will do whatever you ask in my name, so that the Son may bring glory to the Father. You may ask me for anything in my name, and I will do it" (John 14:13–14). If we interpret that statement as a carte blanche affirmation that we will always get whatever we want, we will be disappointed. We have already documented enough cases of unanswered prayer to know that we often do not receive what we ask for.

Some have suggested that this promise applied only to the apostles and not their followers. Interestingly, the apostle Paul, who wrote most of the letters of the New Testament, which are for the church era, did not make any such promises about prayer. Rather, he exhorted believers, "Be anxious for nothing, but in everything by prayer and supplication, with thanksgiving, let your requests be made known to God; and the peace of God, which surpasses all understanding will guard your hearts and minds through Christ Jesus" (Philippians 4:6–7 NKJV). He gave no assurance that our requests will be fulfilled—only that we will have the peace of Christ and the ability to accept whatever God gives us.

Even if we take Christ's promise "I will do whatever you ask" for ourselves, it has certain limitations to it. First, He said that whatever we ask "in my name" we will receive (John 14:13–14; 15:16; 16:23–24). That means that the request must be consistent with His character. He does not lend His good name to just anyone for anything. Some do take it upon themselves, of course, and even do miracles "in His name," yet they are barred from the kingdom of heaven (Matthew 7:22–23).

Second, we are to ask "so that the Son may bring glory to the Father." Our prayers must be free of self-interest and must instead seek the glory and approval of God. The main purpose of prayer is not to get us out of bankruptcy or lessen the pain of an inflamed tumor, although the Almighty is concerned about such matters. The primary motive should be the glory of God and the vindication of His honor.

The example of Christ is instructive. We know that He lived for the glory of God. He pleased the Father, who was glorified at the Son's expense. His life was bathed in prayer, and we have reason to believe that His prayers were answered. The closest He ever came to using a prayer as a means to escape physical and spiritual distress was when He prayed in Gethsemane: "Abba! Father! All things are possible for You; remove this cup from Me; yet not what I will, but what You will" (Mark 14:36 NASB).

Christ had every right to ask the Father for anything; why did He not insist that He be exempted from the impending torture of the Cross? That answer is that *it was God's will that Christ suffer.* The prayer of Gethsemane was the means Christ used to receive the grace and power to do the will of God. Prayer enabled Christ to gather strength to go through with His assignment; it was not the means of delivering Him from it.

The bottom line is that promises such as the one in John 14:13–14 must always be subject to the overriding will of God—a will that may involve pain, injustice, and death, just as it did for our Savior. No promise of deliverance or healing in this life can exempt us from that which we might be called to suffer.

THE GIFTS OF HEALING

Usually we use the phrase "gift of healing," but three times the apostle Paul used the plural, "gifts of healing," to speak about a special endowment of miraculous powers (1 Corinthians 12:9, 28, 30). This use of the plural strongly suggests that there were different gifts of healing. Perhaps, as D. A. Carson suggests, not everyone was getting healed by one person, and perhaps certain persons with one of these gifts could heal certain diseases or heal a variety of diseases at certain times. Perhaps even if one person were to be healed by the gifts of one person at a particular time, this does not mean that a "gift of healing" has been bestowed upon the individual and that he or she should enter a full-time healing ministry.[1] Interestingly, Paul who exercised the gift of healing, left Trophimus sick at Miletus (2 Timothy 4:20). Evidently even his gift could not be used in every situation.

Paul also uses the plural when he speaks of "miraculous powers," indicating the same kind of diversity as in the previous gift (1 Corinthians 12:10). We can surmise that not all miraculous powers are healings; they could include exorcisms or natural miracles.

I shall not argue, as some have, that these gifts passed off the scene with the death of the apostles, though we have already shown that there was a precipitous decline in miracles by the second century. Even so, we would agree that Christ who is the Lord of the church, is able to bestow such gifts according to His will even today.

Rather, I shall plead for the end of abuses by those who exercise their gift of healing, those miracles performed under the guise of Scripture but based on a faulty theology, faulty perception, and faulty methodology.

First, the theology of many of the faith healers assumes that all sickness is of the devil; Christ came to defeat Satan, and thus we can be healed whenever we meet the conditions. Entailed within these assumptions is the cruel notion that if you are not healed, it is your fault: a lack of faith, a lack of appropriating the promises, and, in some cases, a lack of seeking the gift of tongues.

We cannot calculate the widespread devastation this false teaching has brought to tens of thousands of sincere believers who sought healing and did not find it. "God has forsaken me!" A woman wept as she told me that healing was hers to have but she was rejected by God because of lack of faith and unworthy deeds. She represents the countless souls who have accepted this theology, not knowing that it is seriously flawed.

Paul was not healed from his "thorn in the flesh" and came to understand that this affliction (possibly malaria) was God's will for him.

A charismatic writer admitted that unbiblical theology about healing creates heartache and confusion. He writes,

> Bad theology is a cruel taskmaster. . . . Shepherds have to bind up the wounds after the traveling teachers and evangelists are gone and the ravaged sheep are left behind. We cannot therefore, do without an adequate Biblical theology of healing. We need a theology that squarely faces facts; I often tell my students, 'If your theology doesn't fit the facts, change your theology.' Jesus is not, after all, a Christian Scientist.[2]

Yes, bad theology is a cruel taskmaster.

Second, such theology also leads to a distorted perception of the role of the faith healer. I've seen more than a few of them strut the platform, interpreting visions, and giving "words from the Lord" that are passed off on a par with God's Word. "If you know someone who is demon possessed, bring him to me!" one preacher shouted. Another boasted, "I was there when the man died . . . and I was tempted to raise him from the dead!" Within the past week, I heard a television preacher tell his flock that just as God caused the ax head to float in Elisha's day, so God will cause computers to wipe out the debts of those who have great faith in God! There is little doubt that such miracle workers transfer the confidence of the people from the Scriptures to themselves.

I do not mean to characterize all faith healers with such triumphalism, but it is seen too often in too many. Humility seems in short supply simply because the gift of healing is misunderstood, misapplied, and misused. Knowing that sickness makes us vulnerable, we are prone to idolize anyone we think can effect a miraculous cure. And the "healer" is equally prone to believe the adulation of his or her adoring followers.

Finally, we see no evidence in the New Testament that some people began a healing ministry, dispensing healing to those who would come to them. On occasion Peter and Paul healed the sick, but it was incidental to their evangelistic/discipleship ministry. First and foremost, they were not known as healers but evangelists, engaging men and women in dialogue about the Messiah.

Let us keep in mind that God sometimes heals the body but always heals the souls of those who come to Him in humility and faith. "He heals the brokenhearted and binds up their wounds" (Psalm 147:3). To keep our priorities biblical is always our greatest challenge.

We can be grateful that the charismatic movement has challenged all of us to expect greater things from God. But we dare not elevate the so-called "supernatural gifts" above the quest for personal holiness, evangelism, and single-minded discipleship.

NOTES

1. D. A. Carson, *Showing the Spirit: A Theological Exposition of 1 Corinthians 12–14* (Grand Rapids: Baker, 1987), 39–40.
2. Charles Farah, "A Critical Analysis: The 'Roots and Fruits' of Faith-Formula Theology," quoted in *Showing the Spirit,* 177.

$\mathcal{J}$esus, Lord of Death

$\mathcal{A}$merican Baby Boomers still are whining because scientists have not yet developed a cure for death," writes John Kass in the *Chicago Tribune.* We can be quite sure that the whining will continue, for a cure for death is beyond the realm of the scientific enterprise. "Therefore, just as sin entered the world through one man, and death through sin, and in this way death came to all men, because all sinned" (Romans 5:12).

No event is so sobering, so final, and yet so sure. If Jesus is Lord, if He is worthy of our trust, He must triumph here or we shall be forever disappointed. To turn water into wine, to feed a crowd with a lunch, or to open the eyes of the blind makes little difference in the face of that which matters most. The smaller comforts have their place, but it is ultimate questions that matter.

A family is busily preparing a Thanksgiving dinner.

The phone rings; it is the hospital calling to say the father, who was en route, was killed in a car accident just a mile from home. The laughter becomes mourning; the anticipation of joy turns into deep shock and sorrow. What a difference death makes.

We all want to be assured that Jesus will walk with us as we pass through the parted curtain. We want to know that He is committed to us on this side of the grave and beyond. We need the confidence that we can entrust both soul and body to His loving care. We need an ultimate Savior for our coming ultimate experience.

This seventh miracle in John's gospel offers proof that Jesus is not just Lord of this world, but also Lord of the next. He is not just Lord of today, but also the Lord of the most distant tomorrows. He is there when we need Him the most.

"Now a man named Lazarus was sick. He was from Bethany, the village of Mary and her sister Martha" (John 11:1). This was the Mary who sat at Jesus' feet, listening to His words; this was the Martha who was "worried and upset about many things" (Luke 10:41). John continues, "This Mary, whose brother Lazarus now lay sick, was the same one who poured perfume on the Lord and wiped his feet with her hair" (John 11:2).

But death comes into every home, including those in which Jesus is loved. In this account, we see Jesus' heart; we see the tragedy and glory of death; we can see the end, but also the new beginning.

REASONS TO NOT FEAR DEATH

Fear of death is found in virtually all cultures. The inner conviction that in death we leave this life for a conscious existence in the next cannot be eradicated from the human heart. What we need is a guide who can tell us what lies on the other side; we need one who is qualified to lead us to God so that we might be with Him forever.

In this story we are given a glimpse into the home of the grieving sisters and also a glimpse into the heart of Jesus.

We Die Within the Circle of God's Love

The sisters sent word to Jesus, saying simply, "Lord, the one you love is sick" (John 11:3). Surprisingly, He replies to the messengers, "This sickness will not end in death. No, it is for God's glory so that God's Son may be glorified through it" (v. 4). Then John adds this bit of commentary: "Jesus loved Martha and her sister and Lazarus" (v. 5).

Though Jesus loved Lazarus, that did not prevent his death. God's love toward us does not mean we will be spared that experience of passing through the iron gate of death. We might feel forsaken by God, but He is there; His love abides with us into eternity. Our suffering is not inconsistent with the love of God.

Jesus also loved the two sisters. They were concerned about their future; how would the family get along, now that Lazarus, who was probably the sole provider for the family, was gone? As word spread throughout the little village of Bethany, the neighbors shared their concerns.

Incredibly, Jesus, who loved this family, did not hurry to Bethany but stayed where He was. "Yet when he heard that Lazarus was sick, he stayed where he was two more days" (v. 6). The time sequence needs some explanation.

When Jesus arrived in Bethany, Lazarus had already been dead for four days. Let's think through the sequence of events. Just possibly, Lazarus died when the messenger arrived, bringing the news to Jesus. Jesus stayed in the Transjordan for two days, and then He began the two-day trek to Bethany. This would account for the four days.

So Lazarus might not have been living when the messenger arrived back in Bethany. But no doubt the words of Jesus were relayed to Martha and Mary; they must have pondered the assurance of Jesus, who said, "This sickness will not end in death. No, it is for God's glory." How could this promise be reconciled with the reality of their brother's demise?

We can imagine that after the messenger left to tell Jesus, the sisters sat waiting for a miracle. But the clammy sweat of death gathered on their brother's brow. His body was filled with anguish and pain, and at last he passed through the iron gate of death. And, according to custom, his body would be wrapped in a shroud and buried within twenty-four hours.

Can we be sure God loves us even when we face death? Can we be sure that our impending demise does not cut us off from God's love? Can any set of circumstances, including God's delay, cause Him to abandon us?

Paul assures us,

> Who shall separate us from the love of Christ? Shall trouble or hardship or persecution or famine or nakedness or danger or sword? . . . No, in all these things we are more than conquerors through him who loved us.

For I am convinced that neither death nor life, neither angels nor demons, neither the present nor the future, nor any powers, neither height nor depth, nor anything else in all creation, will be able to separate us from the love of God that is in Christ Jesus our Lord. (Romans 8:35, 37–39)

Like Lazarus, we also die within the context of Jesus' love. Our death, even if it should be sooner than expected, does not reflect unfavorably on Jesus' care for us. Indeed, death is the chariot He sends to take us home to be with Him.

We Die Within the Circle of God's Providence

Why did Jesus not hurry to Bethany? Was His decision to wait a heartless response to the urgent cry of His beloved friends? Verbally, He is encouraging—"This sickness will not end in death"—but His actions are confusing. He does not hurry, but lingers, giving Lazarus an opportunity to die and be buried.

After two days, Jesus tells the disciples that they must return to Judea, the territory where Bethany was located. The disciples warn him that the Jews tried to stone him on their last visit in Judea. Jesus, confident that He will be protected by the will of God, reminds them that to walk in obedience is to walk in the daylight, whereas to walk at night is indeed dangerous. To walk without confidence in the will of God would lead to stumbling.

"Our friend Lazarus has fallen asleep; but I am going there to wake him up" (John 11:11). Then Jesus explains that Lazarus was not just sleeping, but that He has died. "So then he told them plainly, 'Lazarus is dead, and for your sake I am glad I was not there, so that you may believe. But let us go to him'" (v. 14).

"I am glad I was not there!"

The words seem out of place. Martha and Mary are weeping, but Jesus is *glad;* the disciples are filled with fear, but Jesus is *glad!* Of course, He is not glad because of sorrow, but glad because of what sorrow does within the human heart.

Why did Jesus not spare Martha her bitter tears? Why was He not moved to action by the sorrow that threatened to break Mary's tender heart? Why did He not speak the word at a distance, and the flush of health return to Lazarus's cheeks?

Spurgeon has given the best answer to these questions, "Christ is not glad because of sorrow, but on account of the result of it. He knew that this temporary trial would help His disciples to a greater faith, and He so prizes their growth in faith that He is even glad of the sorrow which occasions it. . . . He sets so high a value upon His people's faith that He will not screen them from those trials by which faith is strengthened."[1]

The love of God does not necessarily result in health, wealth, and happy relationships. Jesus is touched by the feelings of our infirmities, but He does not shield us from those trials that will develop the qualities He so values. The delays of Deity are not because of insensitivity to our present needs, but because of greater sensitivity to our ultimate needs. There are benefits in those tears.

When He arrives in Bethany, the word spreads and Martha runs to greet Him.

"Lord, if you had been here, my brother would not have died. But I know that even now God will give you whatever you ask."

"Your brother will rise again."

"I know he will rise again in the resurrection at the last day."

"I am the resurrection and the life. He who believes in me will live, even though he dies; and whoever lives and believes in me will never die. Do you believe this?"

"Yes, Lord, I believe that you are the Christ, the Son of God who was to come into the world." (vv. 21–27, dialogue only)

Martha runs back to the house to tell her sister that Jesus has come to town. Mary runs to meet him, saying the same words as her sister: "Lord, if you had been here, my brother would not have died" (v. 32).

"If only ..."

At almost every funeral I've attended, I have heard, "If only ..."

"If only I had convinced him to go to the doctor sooner ..."

"If only he had not been driving that evening ..."

"If only they had not operated on him ..."

"If only ..."

What shall we do with our "if onlys"?

Jesus would tell us that we must believe that these happenstances are a part of God's sovereign purposes and plan. If we could represent all of our "if onlys" as dots on a sheet of paper, we must then draw a circle large enough to encompass all of them. And that circle represents the providence of God.

We do not know the cause of Lazarus's illness. Perhaps it was a disease, a weak heart, or a bad case of the flu. Whatever, these infirmities were the immediate cause of his death; but the ultimate cause was God. He is the one who can take life or prolong it; He is the one who determines the length of our days. That which is out of our control is firmly within His grasp. No sickness, accident, or bolt of lightning can cause our death if God still has work for us to do.

When Jesus saw the sisters weeping, and the Jews who had come along with them weeping, He was "deeply moved in spirit and troubled" (v. 33). They brought Him to the grave.

"Jesus wept" (v. 35).

In those two words, we see most poignantly the humanity of the Son of God. This is proof, if more proof were needed, that the portrait of Jesus given in the Gospels was not manufactured by wild-eyed disciples who were burning with Messianic fever. If anyone had used his or her imagination to write a biography of God in the flesh, all would have thought Him too far removed from our experiences to weep.

If you and I had been making up the story of Jesus, we would have created a dry-eyed Messiah who refused to weep because He understood the eternal purposes of God. Our Jesus would have been above the emotional roller coaster of mere mortals. Tears in our eyes, but not in His.

Yes, Jesus was the Christ, the Son of the living God. He was more than a man to be sure, but a man, nevertheless. If you had taken a sample of His tears, they would have had the same chemical composition as your own. He is touched with the feeling of our infirmities, and He weeps.

"Jesus wept."

"Jesus, once more deeply moved, came to the tomb. It was a cave with a stone laid across the entrance. 'Take away the stone,'" He commanded (v. 38).

"'But Lord,' said Martha, the sister of the dead man, 'by this time there is a bad odor, for he has been there four days'" (v. 39). Would it have been easier to resurrect Lazarus if he had been dead for just one day, or even one hour? Would being in the grave ten years or ten centuries make it more difficult? No, dead is dead, and only God can bring the dead back to life.

"Did I not tell you that if you believed, you would see the glory of God?" (v. 40). For the world, seeing is believing; for those who trust Jesus, believing is seeing.

This verse has sometimes been misused to teach that we can see whatever miracle we want if only we believe and desire to see the glory of God. But again we have to remember that this was a specific promise regarding a specific situation. Jesus was referring to the words He gave to the messenger: "This sickness will not end in death. No, it is for God's glory so that God's Son may be glorified through it" (v. 4). Jesus did not mean that the disease would not be fatal, but that it would end in resurrection. The sisters had reason to believe and see the glory of God.

So they took the stone away. The One who stood at the tomb could have spoken a word and the stone would have been removed to wherever Omnipotence wished to send it. But the Master wills that His friends be a part of the miracle. They could not restore Lazarus to his sisters, but they could take the stone away. We've learned that there are some things we can do and some things only God can do. Blessed are those who can tell the difference.

Then Jesus prayed, saying words that were as much directed toward those who were standing next to Him as to the heavenly Father Himself. The prayer implies that He and His Father had agreed on this plan in the ages long ago. Before He stepped out of eternity into time at Bethlehem, this moment was already a part of the divine plan. Indeed, it was scarcely necessary to pray the words, since the outcome was certain. Let's listen as the Son speaks to His Father.

"Father, I thank you that you have heard me. I knew that you always hear me, but I said this for the benefit of the people standing here, that they may believe that you sent me" (v. 41). The will of the Father and the prayer of the Son were united in one heart and purpose.

Then He called in a loud voice, "Lazarus, come out!" (v. 44).

In the fourth century, Augustine said that it is good that Jesus called Lazarus by name, or else the whole cemetery would have come out of the graves. Jesus was saying, "Lazarus, this way out!" He was directing Lazarus out of the cavern. He wanted to make sure that they knew that this was the same man they had buried four days ago.

"The dead man came out, his hands and feet wrapped with strips of linen, and a cloth around his face. Jesus said to them, 'Take off the grave clothes and let him go'" (v. 44). Again, they become a part of the miracle. Lazarus was embraced by his sisters and his startled friends. If he remembered what death was like, it mattered not at this moment. His fondest memories were drowned in a chorus of celebrations. The God by whose providence he died is the God by whose providence he lives.

We Die Within the Circle of God's Purpose

Why had Jesus stayed away when told that Lazarus was ill? He said that this sickness would not end in death, but that "God's Son may be glorified."

How was the Son of God glorified?

First, *He proved that He has the power to reverse the process of death.* "Where, O death, is your victory? Where, O death, is your sting?" (1 Corinthians 15:55). Remember what we learned in the first chapter: The more clearly we see established laws reversed, the more clearly we see a miracle. A healed Lazarus would have been a great miracle; a resurrected Lazarus is an even greater one. Death has been conquered.

Second, *Jesus desired to build faith in the lives of His followers.* He was glad for what the sorrow accomplished. It proved that He is as good as His word. To quote Spurgeon once more, "He is glad for your sakes that your husband is taken away, that your child is buried; glad that your business does not prosper; He is glad that you have those pains and aches, and that Thou have so weak a body, to the intent that you may believe."[2]

Death is our ultimate opportunity to glorify God. I have a friend in heaven, a fellow pastor, with whom I had a conversation over the phone just days before he breathed his last. He told me that he always wanted the truths he had preached to sustain him till the end. He wanted to die well, for the sake of his church and family.

"Good-bye, Erwin" he said in a whisper, "I will see you in heaven." His death glorified God.

Third, *it substantiated Jesus' claim, "I am the resurrection and the life.* He who believes in me will live, even though he dies; and whoever lives and believes in me will never die" (John 11:25, italics added). When we die, our physical body accelerates the process of decomposition. But the promise is that we will live even though we die. And if we are alive spiritually, we never really die at all. This is not a denial of death (as Christian Science would maintain); it is a recognition that when the physical body dies, the life Jesus gives us guarantees a glorious future existence.

Jesus did not say, "I give resurrection life," but rather, "I *am* the resurrection and the life." The focus is on who He is. Once we see who He is, it is not difficult to believe what He can do. He who has triumphed over physical death has the power to triumph over spiritual death too. Jesus said Lazarus was sleeping, not because the soul sleeps, but because the body "sleeps" until the day of resurrection. And when we are raised, it will not be with a resuscitated body like Lazarus's, which had to die again, but with a glorious body like Jesus', which will never perish. "We shall be like him, for we shall see him as he is" (1 John 3:2).

The resurrection of Lazarus proves that we have a qualified Savior. We do not need a Savior who can just "help" us. We need a Savior who can resurrect us. We do not just need a Savior who helps us when life gets tough; we need a Savior who can help us when life ends. The Resurrection proves that for us, death is transitional, not terminal. When He gives us "dying grace," we are witnesses to His forgiveness and power. Death is a time of transition, not annihilation.

I wish I could have interviewed Lazarus a day after his resurrection. I'm sure he would have told me that he was now free of fear. Tell him that he might be killed and he laughs, "Been there, done that!" No sickness, no disease, no accident could have made him afraid. He had been to Paradise and back and longed to return. And when he died again, his body was put into the tomb awaiting its final glorification.

The experience of Lazarus illustrates the conversion of a sinner. We are dead "in . . . trespasses and sins" (Ephesians 2:1 KJV), and Jesus makes us alive. We are then set free of our grave clothes; that is, we are freed from the debilitating effects of sin and we are invited to sit with Jesus at supper (John 12:1–3).

William Barclay quotes the dying words of Edward the Confessor, "Weep not, I shall not die; and as I leave the land of the dying, I trust to see the blessings of the Lord in the land of the living. We call this world the land of the living; but it would be in fact more correct to call it the land of the dying. Through Jesus Christ we know that we are journeying, not to the sunset, but to the sunrise."[3]

Do *you* believe this?

For Further Consideration

The Denial of Miracles in Modern Liberal Movements

Whenever I see a picture of Jesus on the cover of *Time* or *Newsweek,* I pick up the magazine with misgivings. I know that Jesus will be dissected, analyzed, and stripped of His deity. In the end we shall learn about a Jesus who is not qualified to be our Savior, much less worthy of worship. The man from Nazareth will be putty in the hands of scholars, bent on fashioning Him according to their preference and liking. He will be a no-frills Jesus, reduced to a mere man. He will be an object of fascination, but not adoration.

Do you find your faith shaken when you read that the very existence of Jesus is questionable? For example, in his book *The Gospel According to Jesus,* Stephen Mitchell wrote, "We can't be sure of anything Jesus actually said." Indeed, *Time* quotes German scholar Rudolf Bultmannn as saying that the Gospel accounts are so unreliable that "we can now know almost nothing concerning the life and personality of Jesus."

Why these conclusions?

Let's take as an example the Jesus Seminar, a group of scholars who meet in California to vote on what they believe Christ did or did not say and do. They devised a creative plan for casting their ballots. Each participant drops a plastic bead into a bucket, and the color of the bead signifies the scholar's opinion. *Red* means "That's Jesus!"; *pink,* "Sure sounds like Jesus"; *gray,* "Well, maybe"; *black,* "There has been some mistake."

Their conclusion is that only about 18 percent of the words ascribed to Jesus in the Gospels may have actually been spoken by Him. To no one's surprise, the resurrection of Christ was blackballed, along with all of the other miracles. Only politically correct words and deeds survive.

These left-wing scholars' stated purpose is to change the way people think about Jesus. They have gone public, and national newspapers regularly report their conclusions. They want to "free the Bible from the religious right" and believe that our culture needs a new view of Jesus, a Jesus that speaks to modern concerns, such as feminism, multiculturalism, ecology, and political correctness. This is a Jesus according to the spirit of our age.

Bible believers have nothing to fear from these subjective speculations. In fact, properly understood, these scholars actually strengthen our faith rather than undermine it! Indeed, the Jesus Seminar *is just one more reason to believe that Christ is who the New Testament writers claim He is!*

Let me explain.

First, keep in mind that these radical views are entirely based on the subjective hunches of each scholar; in effect, every decision is made with an unwavering bias against miracles. To quote the exact words of the introduction of *The Five Gospels: The Search for the Authentic Words of Jesus,* a book published by the Jesus Seminar, "The Christ of creed and dogma, who had been firmly in place in the Middle Ages, can no longer command the assent of those who have seen the heavens through Galileo's telescope."[4]

We have seen the heavens, the argument goes, so we can no longer believe in a miraculous Christ. But these "discoveries" are neither historical nor archaeological. Yes, these scholars have extensively studied the life and times of Jesus, but only from the perspective of their view of Jesus as a *mere* man.

Keep in mind that for centuries liberal scholars have tried to separate the historical Jesus (Jesus the mere man) from what they call "the Christ of faith," that is, the Christ of legend and myth. They have tried to peel away all of the miraculous works and claims in the Gospels to find this man, Jesus. But many modern scholars admit that this enterprise has been a gigantic failure. They have ended up with as many different "historical Jesuses" as there are scholars. Rather than writing a biography of Christ, each scholar has, in effect, written a biography of himself! The life of Christ is a mirror in which each scholar sees his own reflection, doubts, aspirations, and agenda.

THE SUBJECTIVITY OF THE SEARCH

The search for the historical Jesus is a kind of Rorschach inkblot test. Since the manuscripts of the New Testament are rejected as authoritative, one's own conception of Jesus is all that matters. Many different portraits of Christ emerge: Some writers picture Him as a countercultural hippie; others, as a Jewish reactionary, a charismatic rabbi, or even a homosexual magician. The famed humanitarian Albert Schweitzer wrote his own biography of Christ and concluded that it was His insanity that drove Him to claim divinity.

In the end, we know more about the authors of these biographies than we do about Jesus! Their dizzy contradictions and subjective opinions have led many scholars to throw up their hands in exasperation and admit that the quest for the "historical Jesus" has ended in failure. The scholars have discovered that the portrait of Christ in the New Testament is a whole piece of cloth; they cannot find the seam in the garment that would separate "the historical Jesus" from the Christ of faith. No razor blade is sharp enough to carve up the New

Testament with any objectivity. Realizing that the search for the "historical Jesus" is futile, many have concluded that the best course of action is simply to say that we know nothing whatever about Him.

In my book *Christ Among Other gods,* I tell the story of the celebrated painting by Burne-Jones, "Love Among Ruins," that was destroyed by an art firm that had been hired to restore it. Though they had been warned that it was a watercolor and, therefore, needed special attention, they used the wrong liquid and dissolved the paint.[5]

Throughout the ages men have tried to reduce the bright New Testament portrait of Christ to gray tints, to sponge out the miracles, to humanize His claims. So far, however, no one has found the solvent needed to neutralize the original and reduce it to a cold, dull canvas. No matter who tries to blend its hues with those of ordinary men, the portrait remains stubborn, immune to those who seek to distinguish between the original and a supposed later addition.

Try as they might, they could not find a purely human Jesus anywhere on the pages of the New Testament. Their subjectivism left them with random bits and pieces that would not easily fit together. They were faced with a clear choice: *Either they had to accept Him as portrayed in the New Testament or they had to confess ignorance about Him.* In effect, they were faced with the stark realization that the Gospel portrait is either *all* true or *all* false. Determined that they would not accept a miraculous Christ, they opted for saying that there might not have been a historical Jesus at all!

Augustine lived before scholars chewed up the

Scriptures according to their personal whims. Nevertheless, even in his day, some people believed what they wanted and discarded the rest. He wrote, "If you believe what you like in the gospels, and reject what you don't like, it's not the gospel you believe, but yourself."

Yes!

THE RELIABILITY OF NEW TESTAMENT DOCUMENTS

If we are willing to treat the New Testament with the same respect given to other ancient documents, we discover that they are reliable eyewitness accounts of the life and ministry of Christ. They confront us with a Christ who claimed to be God and had the credentials to prove it.

In the back of our minds, we might be wondering: Could the disciples have made up the story of Christ? Could the Jesus Seminar have a point when it concludes that a person named Jesus existed and the disciples turned him into the Christ the Messiah? Even if we cannot separate the Jesus of history from the Christ of faith, even if we cannot find the "historical Jesus," still, is it possible that this person's followers were overcome with "messianic fever" and therefore embellished the stories of Christ? Were they capable of turning an ordinary man into a messiah?

No. Either intentionally or unintentionally the disciples could not have invented Jesus. In his book *History and Christianity,* John Warwick Montgomery gives reasons the disciples were incapable of taking Jesus the man and making Him into a messiah of their liking.[6]

First, Jesus, as He is described in the New Testament, differs radically from the kind of messiah anticipated by the Jews of His era. In other words, Jesus was a poor candidate to be "deified."

The late Jewish scholar Alfred Edersheim, of Oxford University, has shown that it was incredible for Christ to proclaim that His desire was not to make Gentiles convert to Judaism but to make both "children of one heavenly Father," and not to put the Law on the heathen but rather to deliver Jews and Gentiles from it and "fulfill its demands for all!"

To quote Edersheim, "The most unexpected and unprepared-for revelation was, from the Jewish point of view, that of the breaking down of the middle wall of partition between Jew and Gentile, the taking away of the enmity of the law, and the nailing it to His cross. There was nothing analogous to it. . . . Assuredly, the most unlike thing to Christ were His times."[7] The Jews of the day expected the Messiah to appear with a sword to break the Roman occupation from the land; some thought He would bring back the remnant of the ten lost tribes and reunite Israel and Judah.

Christ was a bitter disappointment on all accounts. The Jews were not about to accept a Messiah who said, "My kingdom is not of this world" (John 18:36). No wonder the Jewish officials arranged His crucifixion. *If the disciples had wanted to choose a man to make into a messiah, Jesus would not have made the list.*

Second, the disciples were psychologically incapable of taking a man and calling him God. The central tenet of Judaism is "Hear, O Israel: The Lord our God, the Lord is one" (Deuteronomy 6:4). The greatest blasphemy was idolatry, that is, calling a person or thing God. For the disciples to deify a mere man would be contradicting the most basic point of the Law, "Thou shalt have no other gods before me" (Exodus 20:3 KJV).

To break such a commandment would mean that they were, in Montgomery's words, either "charlatans or psychotics." He continues: "Yet the picture of them in the documents is one of practical, ordinary, down-to-earth fishermen, hardheaded tax gatherers, etc., and people with perhaps more than the usual dose of skepticism."[8]

The point is that the disciples had to be convinced that Christ was the Messiah; there was no way they would have taken a mere man and made him into God. His words and His works forced them to conclude that they were in the presence of the Son of God.

NOTES

1. Charles H. Spurgeon, *The Treasury of the Bible* (Grand Rapids: Zondervan, 1962), 2:456.

2. Ibid., 457.

3. William Barclay, *The Gospel of John,* 2d ed., 2 vols., The Daily Study Bible (Philadelphia: Westminster, 1956; Edinburgh: Saint Andrews, 1965), 2:110.

4. Robert W. Funk, Roy Hoover, and the Jesus Seminar, introduction to *The Five Gospels: The Search for the Authentic Words of Jesus* (New York: Macmillan, 1993; San Francisco: HarperCollins, 1997).

5. Erwin W. Lutzer, *Christ Among Other gods* (Chicago: Moody, 1994), 94–95. This book defends the authority of Christ in more detail.

6. John Warwick Montgomery, *History and Christianity* (Minneapolis: Bethany, 1964). This book is a vigorous and convincing presentation of the reliability of the New Testament portrait of Christ.

7. Alfred Edersheim, quoted in Montgomery, *History and Christianity,* 67–68.

8. Montgomery, *History and Christianity,* 72.

For Doubters Only

We have surveyed seven miracles that were described by John that we "may believe that Jesus is the Christ, the Son of God, and that by believing you may have life in his name" (John 20:31). But the greatest miracle comes at the end of the book, when Jesus is miraculously raised from the dead and appears to the startled disciples.

It was the resurrection of Christ that transformed these men into convinced followers of Christ. Read the New Testament accounts, and you will discover that they leave no doubt that the writers understood the difference between fact and fiction. They were well aware that false messiahs had come and gone, and thus were also skeptical of Jesus. But after His own resurrection they were convinced that He was indeed the Christ, the Savior of the world.

"Doubting Thomas," as the disciple is frequently called, reminds us that Christ is accommodating to honest skeptics whose hearts are open to embrace the truth, but who wonder whether the evidence is sufficient. "Doubt" someone has said, "is stumbling over a stone we do not understand." Hardened unbelief kicks at the stone, determined to not believe.

Thomas had a streak of pessimism, a hunch that in the end nothing would ever turn out just right. After His resurrection, Christ appeared to His disciples, but Thomas was absent, probably brooding over his deep disappointment with Jesus (John 20:19–24). He was not the kind of person who was gullible, gripped with "messianic fever," wanting to take a mere man and make him into a God.

The other disciples were saying to him, "We have seen the Lord!" But he said to them, "Unless I see the nail marks in his hands and put my finger where the nails were, and put my hand into his side, I will not believe it" (v. 25).

A week later, Jesus gave Thomas a challenge: "Put your finger here; see my hands. Reach out your hand and put it into my side. Stop doubting and believe." Thomas answered and said to Him, "My Lord and my God!" (v. 27).

Jesus added, "Because you have seen me, you have believed; blessed are those who have not seen and yet have believed" (v. 29).

A Buddhist in Africa who was converted to Christianity was asked why he changed religions. He replied, "It's like this. If you were walking along and came to a fork in the road and two men were there and one was dead and the other alive, which man's directions would you follow?"

If the Jesus of the New Testament had not existed, no one would have invented Him; indeed, no one could have invented Him. When the chief priests and Pharisees sent officers to arrest Christ, they returned empty-handed. When pressed for an explanation, they replied, "No one ever spoke the way this man does" (John 7:46).

He performed enough miracles to convince us.

If you have never trusted Him as your Savior, you can receive Him right now; simply accept His death on your behalf. "Whoever believes in the Son has eternal life, but whoever rejects the Son will not see life, for God's wrath remains on him" (John 3:36).

What a promise!

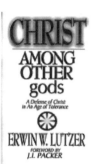

Christ Among Other gods
A Defense of Christ in an Age of Tolerance
Erwin W. Lutzer
1649-7 Paperback

Next time someone claims all religions teach the same basic truths, how will you respond? Here's the factual support you need to defend the primacy of Christ and counter the assertions of Buddha, Krishna, Bahá ú lláh, and Zoroaster. Easily accessible, absorbing answers to the tough questions searching minds are likely to ask.

The Serpent of Paradise
The Incredible Story of How Satan's Rebellion Serves God's Purposes
Erwin W. Lutzer
2720-0 Paperback $10.99

To defeat an enemy, it helps to understand him. Lutzer presents an intriguing overview of Satan's career – his fall from heaven, his work on earth, and his ultimate demise. Discover why God is in control not just of Satan's destiny but of his every action.

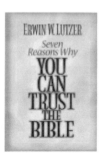

Seven Reasons Why You Can Trust the Bible
Erwin W. Lutzer
8442-5 Hardback $16.99
8444-1 Hardback and Mass set $19.99

Come on a journey of faith where you are asked some of the most fundamental questions any human being could ask: Is there absolute truth? Is belief in Jesus really the only way for us to be reconciled to God? This book will encourage every believer, confirming the changeless truth of Christianity.

Moody Press, a ministry of Moody Bible Institute,
is designed for education, evangelization, and edification.
If we may assist you in knowing more about Christ
and the Christian life, please write us without obligation:
Moody Press, c/o MLM, Chicago, Illinois 60610.